Decent Exposure
Life Stories and Poems

6 Journeywomen

Mountain Wildfire Press

First published in 2003

Mountain Wildfire Press
120 Station Street
Blackheath NSW 2785
Australia

Phone 02 47878784
Fax 02 47876766
Email: sabine@lisp.com.au

National Library of Australia
Cataloguing-in-Publication entry:

Six Journeywomen
Decent Exposure: Life Stories and Poems.

ISBN 0 9579623 2 0

Contributors include Rosemary Morrow, Mira Sonik, Helena Wong,
JosephineWolanski, Alison Gentle and Sabine Erika.

Cover design by Jenny Kee.
Typesetting by Robbie Kenna.
Printed and bound by
Industrial Printing Company, Lithgow, New South Wales

Contents

Acknowledgements

The six journeywomen wish to thank Liz Connor for her scrupulous and sympathetic editing, Robbie Kenna for her dedicated preparation of the manuscript, Jenny Kee for contributing the wonderful cover design, the team at Industrial Printing for their professional assistance and last, though never least, Mira Sonik for the continued use of her kitchen and her care of us all in it.

Foreword

How would it be if you looked back over your life and found fragments of the past to write about? That is what these six writers have done in Decent Exposure. In their stories they have travelled to the far outback, from Latvia to South Africa, from Greenham Common to Bondi Beach, from Medlow Bath to the deep recesses of the mind. In stories they have recreated a past from a present perspective. Some of these women met at Varuna Writers' Centre in the Blue Mountains and have been meeting every week for more than five years to share stories, write, eat and help each other creatively.

Along the way you will find humour and tragedy, commitment and caring, personalities with panache and fighters for freedom.

Readers of the previous book, *Mira's Kitchen*, will recognise some of the characters who people these stories, and some of the places.

The evocative story of her time in the Kimberleys by Rosemary Morrow; the humorous trials of an inner city dweller by Alison Gentle; the warm-hearted fragments of family life from Mira Sonik; the enigmatic Greek personality portrayed by Josephine Wolanski; and the commitment to a sometimes stony path to peace by Sabine Erika. The tales encompass a variety of human experiences, to some of which the reader will undoubtedly relate. These powerful personal images are punctuated by Helena Wong's poetry, which draws from both experience and imagination.

Maybe some readers will be inspired to write, to indulge in some decent exposure of their own.

Six Journeywomen *October 2003*

I'll Go A Little Further: Journey of a Pacifist

Today the war in Iraq began, prosecuted by a 'coalition of the willing'. On the streets of Sydney a large 'coalition of the unwilling' walked in protest. Tonight my sister Monika phoned:

'Say something nice,' she said with tears in her voice.

Thirty-five years ago thousands of Australians took to the streets against the war in Vietnam. It took seven years before the troops came home, men and women who would never be the same again.

Sixty-five years ago my mother, Erika, my father Max, my two sisters, Monika and Renate and I, left Nazi Germany as refugees. War broke out six months after we arrived in Australia and my parents never saw their parents again.

On a shelf in my study is the last photograph taken in Germany. There is my father, young, good-looking, serious, my mother, beautiful, positive, slightly protective behind her mother with whom she had lived alone for many years before her marriage. They had become great friends. My father's parents are also there, grandfather Wohlwill who would lose his life in a concentration camp, also serious, a gifted amateur musician. My grandmother Wohlwill sits there looking warm and friendly. She loved poetry and often laughed. She would return from the camp unable to see. And my grandmother

Overbeck. She was widowed at a young age, wrote in Latin and was an early suffragette. Also in the picture is my father's sister Marguerite, married at 17 to one of her father's fellow musicians. She is pregnant, expecting Mathias who would become another gifted amateur musician and one of four boys of that marriage. The children are not in the photo. I was just a few months old, the third girl in the family.

I remember nothing of Germany, the trauma of the last year, living with the Wohlwill grandparents, the SS raids and the difficulties of getting visas. I do not recollect the decrees that meant that father lost his job, that Jews had to wear stars, that Jewish art works and books were destroyed, that music by Jews could not be played and that all Jewish girls names were changed to Sara and all boys to Israel. I think these names were then attached to their papers so officials would know that they were Jews.

'I remember looking out the window one morning,' my mother recollects from that time, 'as a large black car pulled up at the neighbours and I watched the family being taken away.'

All my life I have been aware of all this, and all my adult life I have been a pacifist.

As a refugee family in a strange country, without relatives, we clung together and our parents were an immensely strong influence, one that I often reflect on now. My gentle father who hardly ever spoke of Germany under the Nazis, and when he did there was no hatred in his voice, nor judgement in his demeanour. I was the fierce pacifist and I used to get annoyed that he was not more outspoken, not angrier or more open with us about what had happened to him, his family and the Jewish people generally. He preferred to tell the story of the kind policeman who would not take his Hamburg registration papers.

'Just go away,' he said to Dad. In this way the Nazi authorities did not know our family were now in Hamburg. My mother was more outspoken. From her we learned something of the tension of those days, the difficulties, and the lengths she had gone to. She said, 'I had to drive because Jews were not allowed to hold a licence and I would find routes which I thought would be safe. Sometimes I had to divert Max's attention from signs on shops, parks and other businesses which said something like *No Jews Here* or *Jews Out*.' My father was unworldly and mother protected him. They were good friends. In an age of temporary marriages I look back on their nearly sixty years together as a miracle marriage.

Almost as soon as we arrived in Australia we met the Quakers, the Religious Society of Friends, and within a couple of years my parents had joined the Society. Quakers subsequently became like an extended family. After my parents, I suppose that Friends became the next great influence on my life and in particular on my peace journey. What a fascinating collection they were. There were the Lembergs, also Jewish refugees, Rudi a scientist and Hannah a craftsperson of great creativity. Then there were the Swan sisters, strict loving spinsters descended from early settlers, who taught us Sunday School and smelled a bit musty when they kissed us. Their clothes were plain as befitted Quakers, and they wore small felt hats and gave enormous energy to the Meeting and its philanthropic work. I remember Dorothy Gregory who had escaped from Shanghai and was a marvellous example of a strong intellectual woman, and Margaret Watts, who had braved the imperial hysteria of World War One to help form the Women's Peace Army, and had been to the Soviet Union.

And every second Sunday my father used to visit Mary Mogine, an elderly Quaker who could no longer travel to Meeting for Worship. In her heyday she had gone out into the streets of Surry Hills in inner city Sydney and gathered up young women, factory workers living in the slums, and brought them to the Meeting House for dancing. Her family were all radicals, working for Aborigines, for peace and for women long before it was fashionable. Even the Quakers thought it a bit much at times.

It was the Quaker peace testimony that in time became a strong element in my life.

In 1660 George Fox, one of the original Quakers wrote to Charles 11:

> *We utterly deny all outward wars and strife and fightings with outward weapons, for any end, or under any pretence whatever; this is our testimony to the whole world ... The Spirit which leads us into all truth will never move us to fight and war against anyone with outward weapons, neither for the Kingdom of Christ nor for the Kingdoms of this world.*

Every subsequent war saw the Friends deliberating about a renewed testimony for peace and many have suffered imprisonment and vilification for their opposition to war. I have not suffered for my beliefs although I have been ridiculed. I remember being called a 'dirty commo' and having rotten tomatoes thrown at me at the university. In many conversations with people who disagreed with my stand I have been charged with ignorance, brainwashing and other less complimentary attributes. I have my own peace testimony, which took many years to emerge. My truth is that there is that of God in every person and therefore life is sacred and cannot be taken under any circumstances. I know that life is taken violently somewhere every day, but I still believe the words of a song we often sang under stress at Greenham Common Women's Peace Camp:

'You can't kill the spirit, it is like a mountain, old and strong it goes on and on and on ...'

I have not been in a war but I believe in this spirit firmly, more each day.

My journey towards this truth has gone along many paths and despite our different approaches, I believe my father has had a strong influence over my journey. He inculcated in me a strong sense of justice and human rights. He saw that of God in everyone. He used to tell a story about his mother whenever we came home with a story critical of someone's behaviour: 'We had a young woman working for us as a housemaid,' he would begin, 'and she became pregnant. When others criticised her, my mother would say, 'Ah but she is simply one of those women who have a baby before they are married.'

My mother gave me a love of life and celebration and modelled for us an enthusiasm for all kinds of people, an enthusiasm which I have inherited and which sometimes leads to disappointment.

'I would rather think the best of someone first, even if I am disappointed later,' my mother would say. 'Rather that than to expect the worst first.'

As well as Quakers, a great variety of people came into our house and my parents always seemed to be able to find a point of contact with them.

I remember Ollie Noisky, a Czechoslovakian refugee, teaching us girls to waltz in the dining room of our old weatherboard house. He was a very large man but as light as an autumn leaf on his feet. I knew dimly that he had experienced terrible things but not what they were. Then there was Margaret Delmar, a fierce-looking Jewish spinster who was utterly opposed to marriage but a great friend to my parents. She was frighteningly clever and always wore black because 'Someone dies every minute somewhere in the world.' She spoke many languages and had the largest collection of newspapers and journals I had ever seen at that time, and we had to make our way through towering piles of them in her Sydney flat. There was Marie Byles, who was rejected by Quakers for her unorthodox beliefs. She was a fierce environmentalist long before it was fashionable and led the struggle for the establishment of Boudi National Park on the North coast of NSW. She was a Buddhist and ate sparingly, unless my mother made a butter cake or a Strosle cake and then she hoed in. In the forties she took us on weed elimination walks in the bush and gave us our first sleeping bags and tent. We made up a limerick about her:

'There was an old woman called Byles,
Who would make us walk miles upon miles.
She would call out 'relax',
We would fall on our backs,
For that crazy old woman called Byles.'

I don't suppose she was really old at that time, except to us children. We helped her build her Hut of Happy Omen in the bushland behind her house and were allowed to stay there sometimes.

There were so many more and no doubt all had some influence upon the young me.

Every month the young Quakers and their friends came to our house. It was the post-war years and there was a ferment of discussion about socialism, pacifism and all kinds of politics. Most of it passed me by, I was too young to appreciate it, but some rubbed off. I remember one man, Ted Hartley, who had been to jail as a conscientious objector, and the Morris sisters who did interesting things, teaching at a correspondence school and connecting with the outback through the School of the Air. Herbert Menka was another Jewish refugee who enjoyed the company of Young Friends and who met his Australian wife, Margaret, in our house, through my matchmaking mother. And then there was the young and fiery Arthur Lukes, who met and married a French woman and had his reception in a milk bar.

I wanted to be an actor and I joined the Studio Theatre in Sydney as a ten year old. Dennis Glenny, an actor with the Anthroposophical Theatre, attracted me immediately. He was larger than life, a bear of a man with the most generous personality and a wonderful fruity actor's voice. He used to escort me to Wynyard Station from the seedy depths of Hamilton St. He was my protector, and became a great friend and godfather to my first son, Simon. During World War 11 he joined a performance unit and entertained the troops. He had been at the Royal Academy of Dramatic Art (RADA), was a pacifist and would not have been able to fight. My parents loved Dennis, and mother, who always had a weakness for gentle men, had a signed theatrical photo of Dennis pinned to the inside door of the hall cupboard. I have missed him since he died.

I was married with two sons, Simon and Anthony, when the Vietnam War began. It was 1968. I had just started studying at the university. My husband, David, had been a conscientious objector to National Service in the fifties and had served six months in military jail because of it. It was one of the things that attracted me to him. We both opposed Australia's involvement in this war and helped form a local Moratorium Group. It was heady stuff. We held meetings, leafleted the area and sought publicity for our cause in the local newspaper. One of the most energetic workers was Jane Gray, a staunch campaigner for human rights and public education.

'Hullo Jane, guess what? Jim Cairns has agreed to address our next public meeting.' Jim Cairns was at that time a highly regarded politician. He subsequently published a book on Vietnam peace politics called *Silence Kills* and I have always found that expression an inspiration. Our meeting was a great success. The hall was filled to overflowing and even a question about the absence of public toilets in the area elicited a gracious answer from Cairns.

We signed petitions, held vigils and took part in the huge marches in the city. The first march I attended was held on a blustery winter day. I took the children and had to stop on Broadway at a disposal store to buy them each a duffle coat. The march turned nasty. The police had instructions to stop us. 'Ride over the bastards,' the then Premier, Robert Askin had said, and that's almost what they did. Many people were hurt and many were arrested. Shop windows were broken and fences destroyed. I never took the children again.

The Vietnam War was a turning point for many people. It certainly was for me. The Cold War atmosphere, the recent McCarthy-ite hysteria and what I call the gravity theory of history, ie that the reds would trickle down the map to Australia, meant that for many people our opposition amounted to treason at worst, a communist plot at best. It was during these times that I encountered the skinheads, or Neo-Nazis. I had not realised before that there were people who wanted to emulate the Nazis, and even re-write history to persuade people that the Nazi crimes never occurred. Sometimes we thought our phones were tapped and as though to confirm this two secret police arrived on our doorstep early one morning. It was as though Laurel and Hardy had arrived to interrogate us. One of them asked the questions, the other wrote down the answers. There was really only one question they were interested in, 'Who put you up to it?' The scribe had great difficulty with his task, bit his pencil and scratched his ear in perplexity at any unfamiliar words that we used to recount the history of Vietnam and its struggles, words like 'accords' and 'struggle' and 'independence'. I've often wondered what those two made of the session in our timber-lined kitchen and how it was reported back to head office. Did we seem like dangerous commie spies to them?

At Macquarie University, where I was studying history, philosophy, and English literature and language, we formed an anti-Vietnam group and held teach-ins to inform ourselves about the situation. A growing number of people opposed the conscription by birthday ballot of 18 year olds, old enough to be killed but not old enough to vote. I took a petition around the staff. It was my first experience of the direct solitary approach. So many refused to sign, especially those from economics and accounting. Those who signed and supported us stand out like lights. There was Jill Roe, a lecturer, now Professor of History and an inspiration to hundreds of students, Max Deutscher, Professor of Philosophy, at that time the youngest professor in Australia, immensely intelligent and a bit awe-inspiring for new students. And there was the Professor of Physics, Peter Mason, a brilliant man whose scientific work never obscured or neglected the importance of politics. Our fiercest opponents at the university were the self-styled rugger buggers who disrupted our campus meetings with shouts and missiles. But it was also there that I first felt the strength of a support group, a few staff amongst them.

More and more I was enjoying the company of women, strong women who increasingly rejected the stereotypes assigned to us for generations. This obsession with women's liberation, with feminism, heralded another turning point in my journey.

It sat a bit uneasily with my marriage but I did not want to think about it at this time.

One day the phone rang. It was Marie Tulip, another peace worker and poet, ringing to ask if I could join a Council of Churches Women's Commission representing Quakers. Though somewhat bemused I agreed to give it a go. On my way home from my first ever women's conference, I dreaded returning to my everyday life. I sat in my Volkswagen and cried. Who would understand the extraordinary experience I knew I had had? Certainly not a man and two boys, loving as they were. The Commission and the Conference, Women's Liberation and the Church, turned out to be a great experience for me both in terms of my peace journey and my adventures into feminism. I became a member of Mothers and Others for Peace and the Magdalene collective. Magdalene was a monthly magazine devoted to issues related to women and the church. We tackled everything from theology to sex via domestic violence. It was the issue of domestic violence that gradually brought together the two strands in my life, feminism and pacifism.

I loved women, I wanted to work with women and I was so naïve about many of the issues that affected our lives. My own happy childhood with its absence of violence combined with the apparent naivety of my parents left me totally unprepared for the shock of domestic violence and rape. These two issues were of great concern to the women's movement. I thought at first that issues like equal pay and access to important jobs were where the struggles were at. But I soon learned differently. Violence against women was widespread and cruel. I discussed this with my mother. She couldn't believe it. 'Surely not,' she would say. 'People don't behave like that.' Sadly, they do. I did not discuss this issue with my father. I think I unconsciously followed my mother in protecting Dad from the less lovely aspects of modern life. Mum used to say, 'Max does not really belong in this world'. To me domestic violence seemed like a war against women, not only the violence itself, but the silence around it, the acceptance of it, and the widespread belief that it was often the woman's fault. I was a convert to the cause.

We set up a task force on domestic violence and the church. Yes, even behind the parish walls this violence was not uncommon. We were told sad stories. 'No one believed me,' one woman told us, 'because my husband was a minister. They said I should have counselling, that I was probably stressed.' Another woman told us how she was believed but that the man she went to for help only offered to pray with her and told her that she must stay with her husband and be his helpmeet.

'It is your duty as a wife, you must try harder to please him,' he concluded. 'I tried everything,' she said. 'He still hit me hard, but not where it would show.'

At a general meeting of the Australian Council of Churches we launched our video on domestic violence and the church, with an accompanying kit for use in churches. It was a sobering experience, and an uncomfortable one for many who were there. One brave woman got up and talked of her experience as a victim. This had a powerful effect, especially on the doubters. I felt brave and sad and excited that we had done this work. I had never done anything like it before and I believed at that moment that I could do anything. A presentation to Quakers disabused me of this pretty quickly. After showing the video and speaking briefly to it, a man rose and spoke fiercely: 'Why are you wasting time on this? You should be working on child abuse.' Many people thought that issues related to women were unimportant.

I disagreed!

By 1975 I had left my marriage, completed my studies, and begun teaching as a tutor at Macquarie University. I began in Reformation history but was soon involved in the new Women's Studies course. 'Women and history, there's no such thing,' one of my colleagues declaimed at a School meeting when this new course was proposed. When it was finally approved and set up by Janet Ramsay, it was hugely popular. We were longing to know our own history, and to write it. Without a history we were like someone without a memory, and so many women in our past had done so much. Eventually I set up my own course, 'Women, Politics and Power', which gave me an opportunity to explore the issues of violence and power more closely. And many of my students did major research projects in these areas. Not a few had first-hand experience of violence. It remains one of my most moving experiences to have been entrusted with so many stories, and one of my most exciting experiences to see these women name their pain and discover their own power to be more fully themselves. These years at Macquarie University were full and challenging, although I was never a proper academic. I did some research on militarism and masculinity and then one day I picked up a feminist magazine from Canberra and there was an advertisement for an Anzac day rally at the War Memorial to remember women raped in war. It was to be the occasion of my first arrest, and it happened like this.

I drove to Canberra, nearly four hundred kilometres away with a friend, Carol Allport. We were excited and nervous. It was a bold thing that we were doing, demonstrating about rape in war in front of returned service people and their families, and on that sacred of days, Anzac Day. This day commemorated the Gallipoli Battle of World War One, the day, so our history books told us, that Australia came of age, and achieved true nationhood. Carol and I joined the crowd of women, several hundred strong, in a park close to the War Memorial Drive where the parade would pass. We gathered on the road and began our walk, and when a wall of police officers ordered us to stop, we sat down on the road and conferred. It was agreed that we would disperse and regroup closer to the Memorial. I walked off up the side of the road towards the Memorial alone, feeling brave and strong. Suddenly a policeman stepped in front of me:

'Turn round and go back,' he said.

'Why?' I asked. 'There is no law against walking up the pavement.'

'Turn around,' he ordered.

I kept walking. He arrested me and marched me off to a waiting paddy wagon. 'What is your name?' I asked him, remembering how in the Vietnam days officers had pulled their numbers off to prevent identification.

'Sergeant Charge,' he replied. I was more than sceptical and truly surprised when later in court it turned out he was indeed Sergeant Charge!

We were charged with 'Behaviour likely to cause offence at an Anzac Day Parade' in contravention of a bylaw hastily passed a few days before the parade. At the subsequent hearing the case was dismissed.

I returned to Sydney buzzing with ideas. Next year we should have a similar action in Sydney. That's where the parade was biggest and we would have most impact. I was apprehensive and determined all at once, and before long I had gathered around me a great group of women similarly determined. We gave each other courage. We began to publicise the plan and held meetings in the city Quaker hall to discuss our strategy. From the outset we decided that it would be a silent and non-violent action. We started training in non-violence. Every woman contributed. Some ran the training, and some designed the logo for our poster and T-shirts, a striking black wreath with the words 'In memory of all women raped in all wars' inside. We became SWARC, the Sydney Women Against Rape Collective and started to receive some publicity. Our own research revealed what we already knew, that rape was an integral part of war, an act of violence encouraged by the training for war and by military life. People begged us not to do it, or at least to hold it on another day. We were committed.

The Sydney Rape Crisis Centre held a phone-in and heard tragic stories, some from women who had never talked before.

'I've never told anyone this, but one day a strange serviceman stood on my doorstep. "Your husband said to come," he said. I thought making him welcome was the least I could do. He raped me, over and over, saying, "Bill said it would be OK." I never felt the same about my husband again.' In Vietnam the nurses were often fearful of their own allied men. Another dimension of 'friendly fire'.

Years later I read in an account of interviews with Vietnam veterans how rape made one man feel, 'I felt like God, I could do anything'. In the accounts of the Soviet advance on Germany in 1945, there are stories of how the soldiers proceeded rape by rape. Everywhere the war against women was evident, at home and abroad.

In the spirit of non-violence we decided to approach the police for permission to hold our walk. Permission was denied and we went to court. On one side of the court sat the suits, police and RSL officials, a sober sight. On the other side sat the women, colourful and animated, taking turns to go out and do child care duty. Three of us were the applicants, Rosemary Pringle, Lynette Ariel and myself. In court we were told we were like strangers at a funeral, that Anzac Day belonged to the RSL and that we were welcome to gather at another place on another day. We lost our case and were denied permission to march. But we were determined to continue.

On the 25th April 1983 a crowd of several hundred women gathered in a small Sydney park not far from George Street, where we would begin our march approximately one hour earlier than the Anzac Day parade. We wore black for mourning and sang that moving Judy Small song, 'It's not only Men in Uniform Who Pay the Price of War.' Standing watching us was a small crowd of onlookers, mostly supportive, including a couple who asked if they could walk on the pavement alongside us in memory of their daughter who had also been raped and killed.

Presently we walked up Bridge Street, silently and slowly as agreed. We carried at the front a large banner that read 'In Memory of all Women Raped in all Wars'. As we rounded the corner into George Street we saw, lined up at the first intersection, a huge band of police, more of them than of us. We continued slowly and silently. A few of the women withdrew onto the pavement. The atmosphere was tense but peaceful. In our training we had rehearsed this so many times – no violence, either physical or vocal, no resistance, just our combined strength which was hugely powerful. I have only experienced this transforming power a few times in my life and I would not have missed it for anything. Maybe some people feel it when they climb mountains, I don't know, but it's an overwhelming thing.

As though we had all communicated, in a sense I suppose we had, we stopped a couple of feet away from the towering wall of police and formed ourselves into a tight circle, holding hands and facing outwards. The arrests began: 180 women, myself included, were taken to the bare and grubby city cells. Like all of us, I was charged with 'Causing serious alarm and affront'. We had to wait to find out how we had done this.

In court a month later our tiny barrister, Deirdre Connor, questioned the police closely. Who was alarmed? Who was affronted? One officer vowed she had seen one of the demonstrators baring her bottom. On closer questioning it was revealed that the officer was on the train going home before our walk started. Our barrister also queried the possibility of these experienced police being so easily alarmed and affronted. The case was dismissed and a cheering crowd awaited us outside the court. We repaired to a local café to celebrate.

A few weeks later I left for England and the greatest adventure of my life. It was my first study leave from Macquarie University and I was going to Oxford to pursue my interest in 'Masculinity, mateship and militarism.' But first I was going to Rome to meet my new lover, and the world was singing. Romance and Rome, what a heady combination! She was my first woman lover and as I waited for her by the Spanish steps, my heart thumped agreeably. How many lovers have met here I wondered, and from how many parts of the world? Moo was enamoured with the ancient goddesses, and we wandered from one museum into another to find these creatures. Had I not been so besotted I would not have followed this pursuit so enthusiastically, I don't like museums much. They make me very tired very quickly. But the reward came later as we settled happily into a little convent in the 'Street of the Artists'.

Inevitably and relentlessly the time came close for me to go on to Oxford and Moo to continue her gypsy wanderings in the USA. In my grief, not only over her departure, but what was really the end of the affair, I consoled myself with the idea of a quick trip to Comiso in Sicily where I had heard there was a Women's Peace Camp alongside an American missile base. But first, after seeing Moo off, I sat down on the floor in the departure hall at Heathrow and howled out loud. The English, who have seen everything in an Empire on which the sun never set, ignored me. I howled all the way in the tube to Bloomsbury and all the way into the travel agents to buy my ticket to Comiso for the following morning.

Around Italy women in the peace movement had combined to buy land alongside the base in Comiso. I came in by bus one afternoon and enquired of a passing police officer where the base was located. He called over a chap who was just about to take off on a bike and asked him to give me a ride, at least that is what I presumed he said. My Italian was less than basic. I hopped on happily, pack on my back and we took off. I became uneasy as the ride seemed to be taking a long time and we were going further and further into the countryside. Suddenly he stopped, jumped off and started to pull me off to give me a kiss. I declined, he pulled and pulled, I resisted. Suddenly I exploded. 'Get on the bike at once and take me to the base,' I commanded in English, and he did, somewhat grumpily.

The women were wonderful, they welcomed me and made me a large mug of tea. I stayed a few days and learned something of the great difficulties for Italian women in acting so independently. 'My family wont talk to me any more,' one woman told me, 'until I come home and find a husband.' 'Some of the women here have been arrested under a sixteenth century prostitution law and are still in prison,' another woman said. 'They are treated very badly there.' It seemed that independent women had no status, especially in Sicily. Transforming power worked once more in Comiso. One morning as I sat quietly in the outside loo I looked up to find a man waving a rifle in my direction. I called out to the women who, as one, encircled him and began to sing; as they sang they walked him slowly off the land.

I was quite sad to leave this courageous group but looked forward to the hallowed halls of Oxford.

'Excuse me miss, we don't dress like that here.'

'We do in Australia,' I replied. I discovered that this fellow, who reminded me of Virginia Woolf's Beadle, was referring to my trouser legs, which I had tucked into my socks for warmth. The colleges of Oxford were bitterly cold and Queen Elizabeth House, the college for visiting colonials, was no exception.

It was brilliantly situated, close to the centre of this ancient scholastic town. I loved to walk about the old streets and imagine a former time, for I was bitterly disappointed in the present. In those grand old buildings lived some very ordinary people – the men were sexist and the women barely tolerated, clinging to the edge of an archaic institution, a privileged institution whose reputation was no longer deserved. I realised that Australian men, whom I had thought were probably the most sexist in the world, were actually much more acceptable than the English men I encountered at Oxford. There they did not even notice you. Try getting served in an Oxford pub for instance. In Australia you knew where you were, even if that was knee deep in pigshit.

I attended my seminar and spent happy times with the other two visiting 'fellows', Barbara from the States, and Wanjira from Kenya. But I was restless, anxious to go to Greenham Common where hundreds of women were camped in opposition to the American nuclear missile site. I had heard and read quite a bit about this camp. The year before, 1982, a Welsh woman Anne Pettit had gathered forty women and four men and started to walk from Cardiff in Wales to Newbury in England where Greenham Common was, to protest against the missiles. She called the march 'Women for Life on Earth'. On the way many others joined her and on arrival at the Common they decided they would stay there until the missiles were removed - it took ten years. Meanwhile it became a women's peace camp where women from all over the world came bringing many concerns related to peace and non-violence. The decision to make it a women's camp had been taken for a variety of reasons. Working in the anti-Vietnam and peace movements had shown these women that men always wanted to take the lead, with women relegated to the secretarial and tea-making functions. Moreover, men seemed more prone to violence both towards women and amongst themselves. It was also hard for many men to move away from 'the woman as sex object' frame of mind, and as well women just wanted a women-only space where they could just be themselves. I resolved to join them.

One morning I boarded a bus for Newbury, nervous and excited. As Oxford disappeared behind me I focussed on my new adventure, working out in my head how I would approach the place and the people. The welcome I had received in Comiso reassured me that it would not be too difficult to arrive as a stranger at Greenham.

The reality was different. The bus driver and his passengers were no longer friendly when I asked the way to Greenham – I learned quickly that the campers were loathed in Newbury. The American servicemen on the other hand were much loved as big spenders and potential protectors. From what, I often wondered?

The last part of the journey was on foot, along the road and into the Common along a path gently wooded on either side, and inexpressibly English. How different from the grandness and the grey-green of the Australian bush. It was November and a few autumn leaves still clung to the trees and it was very cold. I was glad to see a wisp of smoke and a sign that said *Greengate*, one of the many camps situated around the nine-mile perimeter of the base. I followed a narrow track to a clearing, where there was the fire and some women, at last.

'I'm Sabine,' I said, 'from Australia.'

'Yeah. The kettle's on the fire, help yourself to tea if you want.' I did.

I subsequently discovered that the women had decided to dispense with the polite formalities drummed into most women at an early age. So many visitors came to Greenham since the huge publicity in the media, most of it negative, that the women would have spent their whole time caring for guests. I soon came to appreciate this approach, although I found it hard at first to ignore deeply ingrained habits.

Life at Greenham soon became my reality. I could not really visualise myself either at Oxford or back in academe in Australia. I stayed on and off for three months, the most challenging time of my life.

In my mind what stands out from this time is the friendship, the cold, and the struggle for peacefulness. There were women from all over the world, women experienced in the peace movement, fierce socialist women, women escaping from intolerable and violent situations, women from wealthy and comfortable backgrounds and women from the struggling poor of England. We had to learn to work together both with the women at Greengate and with the women camped at the other gates. Imagine large groups of women many of whom were strong and stroppy. Our time was often spent around the fire talking out our differences, trying to see the way forward. It was not always easy as some women thought that violence could and should be countered with more violence. Some used violent language, especially those who had lived in violent situations. It was hard for them but we all persisted. What I soon realised was that there is a bit of violence in all of us and that it's quite hard to let go of it.

As well there were the stresses of living in uncomfortable and cold conditions. There was the constant surveillance from the soldiers and military police. There were the strong base lights turned our way at night, illuminating the forest in which we camped. Our tents were made of thick plastic, we called them benders, and the lights shone through them making weird shadows and often beautiful shapes. Getting up for a pee in the night was a challenge, both because of the cold and the lights. At any time, day or night, low-flying helicopters flew above us malignant and menacing, blowing our belongings and our benders and raising the dust. For me it always felt like a war zone reminiscent of Vietnam War footage. And then there were the raids by local Council trucks scooping up women's belongings because we were not supposed to be there. As we tried to expose the evils of nuclear missiles, we ourselves were laid bare. We were like the witches of old in Newbury, not burned or drowned, just persecuted and loathed, maybe even feared?

'Who are the witches?
Where do they come from?
Maybe your great-great-grandmother was one.
Witches are wise wild women they say,

There's a lot of witch in every woman today.'

We sang this at Greenham.

A day at Greenham had its own rhythms. I soon slipped into the routine. I had to walk around the base and visit the other gates and the women who were camped there. Greengate camp was considered the most radical. I had heard about it and was naturally attracted there. Yellowgate was the musical camp, and multicoloured Maingate, was the general meeting place. It had the only standing pipe, our sole water supply until Newbury Council removed it. Maingate was the first stop for visitors, and recipient of all mail delivered to the women. The campers at Maingate experienced the most harassment as they were the most exposed to the public. Around the other side of the base from us were Bluegate and Redgate. Bluegate attracted the support of a group of county ladies. Every few weeks they drove up in their immaculate sedan and unloaded a huge hamper from the boot for the women. The hamper was filled with the most delicious food, which may even have come from Harrods and was a welcome break from beans and billy tea.

The first challenge of the day was washing, oneself as well as any clothes. We had built a washstand for washing up as well as other washing. It reminded me of Girl Guide camps, three sticks lashed together, a basin perched on top. The water was cold and if no police or military were hovering I could strip to the waist and wash the top part, cover up quickly and do the rest. If I was first up I could light the fire and put the kettle on for tea. Everything took a long time. The benders might need attention, wood needed to be collected and water fetched. After we lost the Maingate water supply we had to fetch water elsewhere, sometimes from Newbury.

A visit to Maingate took place each day to collect water, mail and messages. Maingate was the communications hub. Visitors often came there first and we would encounter groups and individuals from all over the world. My knowledge of German came in handy. I was thrilled one day when a letter came from a group of German schoolchildren telling us they had walked around their shopping centre in support of us at Greenham and of peace. They wrote: 'You must be very strong women because we saw you on TV being stronger than the police.' They enclosed some chocolate for us, and pictures of themselves with banners of support. We received letters of support and donations from all over the world. Sitting down and reading the mail was certainly a highlight.

'Dear women at Greenham,' wrote one correspondent, 'what you are doing is remarkable. I feel you are doing it for me and for my children. I wish I was there with you but I cannot manage. I am with you in spirit and I love you all.'

My mother wrote and asked me to buy a tree to plant on the Common, she also enclosed a bundle of candles for us. We found a snow gum and planted the tree with much ceremony. In stones around it we wrote her name, Erika. Years later I found the tree again, spindly but much taller, and proud of its place on the liberated Common.

At Maingate there were tents with artists, writers and media people. We spent a lot of time composing press releases to inform the world of what we were doing. Most of the reports in the papers were pretty bad, certainly initially. Gradually a grudging admiration crept into the reports as people realised that these women were peaceful, and determined to stay in spite of the bad conditions. Much time was also spent planning actions, learning non-violence, walking around the base, going into Newbury to buy supplies and doing basic maintenance. I constantly marvelled at the ingenuity, the bravery and the sheer panache of women. A large group had crept into the base one night and danced on a missile loader. It was a beautiful picture. What a contrast! They also captured a sentry box for 24 hours and sang peaceful songs to the perplexed guards.

It was not easy under all these adverse conditions to be and remain peaceful. Some of the women believed that all police and military were evil. We talked about this a lot. There were groups of English police camped around the outside of the base and we decided that it would be good to make contact with them. So we went daily and held friendly conversations and shared humorous experiences with them whenever this was possible. We warmed ourselves at their fires and found our mutual humanity made it possible for us to see beyond their uniforms and their designated roles, and for them to see us as something other than hairy-legged, radical lesbian feminists.

Around the campfire and on our walks around the base we shared many hundreds of stories, particularly of peaceful actions and peaceful resolutions of conflict. I learned of the violence many women experienced in their lives and the difficulty they had in imagining peaceful outcomes. I shared a story I had heard from an Army Officer who had worked with paratroopers trained for work in Ireland.

'These men,' he said, 'have been trained not to communicate with *the enemy*, whoever that happens to be at any time.' At Greenham we were the enemy of course.

'They only grunt while they are attacking,' he concluded. 'The tragedy is that they are eventually unable to form any relationships. Their marriages and other relationships break down.'

I think our mutual story-telling helped us to build a peaceful community, but most important was experiencing the strength of non-violence through actions we were involved in. No amount of talking could convey as much as one action. For me, and I believe for many others, this was the decisive factor.

One day as we sat around the fire two military officers appeared and walked up to me.

'You are Sabine Willis?'

'Yes.'

'You will come with us.'

The women surrounded us. 'Where are you taking her?' one asked.

'To Newbury Police Station,' they lied.

They put me onto a truck and took me onto the base where I was led into a small room and interrogated for two hours.

'Are you Australian? Were you in London two days ago? Why are you here? Who suggested you come?' And so it went on. To every question I replied, 'I have nothing to say.' Even to my own nervous ears I sounded like a broken record but I felt strong knowing that the women supported me even though they were not there.

After dark they drove me about a mile away from the base and dropped me by the roadside. I walked back and at last arrived at the track leading up to Greengate camp. In the dim light I saw a figure sitting on a stump by the side of the track. As I came up to her, I saw that it was one of my fellow campers waiting for me, and it was the best welcome I have ever experienced. The women had been to Newbury and discovered I wasn't there. But they'd bought a bottle of Baileys Irish Cream to celebrate my return.

Stories and actions, talking and friendship, these were the elements of life at Greenham. There were some wonderful women there, including a woman I knew from Australia. Katrina was a doctor who spent a lot of time at Greenham and some time in jail. She was a great bushie and knew how to wield an axe or a saw with considerable skill. Many of the inner city women were so out of their element. They had never camped, never cooked on or made a fire, never squatted over a hole in the ground or washed in cold water. At least I'd had some bush and camping experience.

Close to us were camped the Grandmothers for Peace. After an incursion into the Base through a hole cut in the fence these amazing women would weave shut the holes with all the calm and confidence of experienced sock-darners. If women were caught cutting the holes they would be dragged through them, care being taken to scrape any bare parts of their bodies against the barbed wire. Some nasty gashes were the result. Greenham Base was a violent place.

In contrast, and despite our differences and the endless provocations, the peace camp survived relatively peacefully for ten years.

One day we heard that the missile carriers were coming out for a practice run. We decided to lie on the ground outside the gate in the form of a spider's web. We were joined only by a woollen thread. The guards came and looked. The police came and looked. And they seemed puzzled. There was no attempt to drag us off or throw us about as was their usual way. We lay in peace, if quaking inside, and they stood in peace. It was transforming power again. We stopped the loaders for that night with only a woollen web.

For much of the time I was there we were planning an action we called Black Cardigans. Black Cardigans stood for bolt-cutters, which we planned to use to liberate the Common by cutting down the nine-mile perimeter fence It was planned for Halloween afternoon, 1983. We agreed to spread ourselves around the Base in small groups and have picnics, sing songs and play. At 4 pm we would begin to cut down the fence.

The day arrived. Had our plans been discovered? More than likely, as about 2000 women were involved and discussions had been going on all over Britain. We dispersed to our picnic spots and ate our cakes and sweets. At 4 pm we began to cut. Oh what a glorious feeling! I was up on the shoulders of my tall Australian friend, Katrina Allen, with the best bolt-cutters imaginable. I had travelled all the way to London to buy them and I remember the indulgent, slightly amused look of the salesman as I purchased them. They cut through the barbed wire like a surf ski through water.

We let out a triumphant shout as our section of the fence came down. As it did the police inside the fence rushed over and knocked me off Katrina's shoulders. I fell on my nose and tears came to my eyes. We were dragged off onto the base, bolt-cutters confiscated by the police. I never saw them again. They were my property and I loved them.

With dozens of other women I was arrested and taken to Newbury to be charged with 'Criminal damage to Her

Majesty's property'. It took hours for us to be processed, and every few minutes more women were brought into the holding pen. We heard at midnight that four and a half miles of fence had been cut down.

'Could I have an aspirin, or something,' I asked a woman officer. My nose was very sore. She gave me some water.

The Press had a field day. My son was in London the day after the action. It was morning and in the Quaker Centre where he was staying an old man was reading the Times. On the front page was a photo captioned: 'Woman in arms bolt cutters in hand'.

'That's my mother,' Simon exclaimed. The old man put his hand in his pocket. 'Well, give her this to buy a new pair of bolt-cutters,' he said.

A few of us subsequently travelled to London where a friendly lawyer gave us advice on conducting our own defence. In court we confidently asked to see the police notebook and discovered that we were described as wearing black, with shaved hair. While many of the women did have shaved hair, mine was long and in a plait. We had quite a bit of fun questioning the police about their pretty simplistic notebook entries. I went on to argue that, far from damaging the common, we were freeing it for the people to whom it belonged, that we were acting for peace. We lost and were fined. Those of us who believed we were not guilty refused to pay the fines and were eventually picked up and taken to Holloway Women's Jail where scrubbing floors was the main activity. I managed to leave for Australia before I was picked up. Many English women from Greenham who have done time in jail formed a support group for women incarcerated in Holloway and Cookham Woods. They write letters, supply soaps and cosmetics and provide some friendship to these forgotten women.

Greenham wasn't just a women's peace camp. It was a movement across the world, which spun off into a great variety of peace-making initiatives in health, welfare education and many other areas. I returned to Australia in 1984 with a Greenham spirit although I did not know where or how I would use it in the future.

The same year I met Myra, and I have been with her for nearly 20 years. My family have reacted to this part of my life's journey in a variety of ways. My younger son, Anthony, thought it rather fashionable to have a lesbian mother, and was happy to introduce me to his student friends. I felt a bit like a rather rare species of bird, a happy state. Simon, my other son, lived in London and when he did get to meet Myra was rather impressed. Both sons seem to have inherited their grandfather's non-judgemental characteristic, but one never knows the reality of other people, perhaps especially our own children's. It was hard for my sister Renate but her generous spirit has always prevailed. Monika and Christopher, my other siblings, seem to accept what is without discussion. I have never forgotten my mother's reaction years before when I began my relationship with Moo. I was visiting one day.

'Something has happened to you,' she said. 'What is it?'

'Nothing, nothing has happened.'

She pressed me further. She always seemed to know. Eventually I told her.

'I have fallen in love with a woman.'

'You are very lucky,' she said. 'This will broaden your outlook and experience of life.'

The years which followed were years of building a relationship, teaching and travelling. Myra and I toured the outback and Eastern Europe. I went to Cockburn Sound and Pine Gap on peace camps. Mother came with me to Pine Gap and I have in my mind a picture of her at 80 sitting in the desert outside the base, with an Aboriginal woman similarly aged, comparing notes.

'I have nine grandchildren,' mother said proudly.

'I have twenty-eight,' her companion quietly replied.

At Pine Gap another Judy Small song was sung.

> *'It rises in the desert*
> *Silver dome upon the sand*
> *Surrounded by the wire*
> *Like a blight upon the land*
> *And the people of the dreaming*
> *Whose sacred land it is*
> *Wonder who this Uncle Sam might be*
> *To think it could be his.*

I continued to teach Women's Studies at Macquarie University and in 1989, after buying a house with Myra in the Blue Mountains west of Sydney, I took a year off from the university to work for the National Domestic Violence Education Campaign in Canberra. It meant living there for a year. We worked with communities all over the country, black and white. We heard many stories. Sitting in the sand with Aboriginal women in Alice Springs we heard of the heartbreak of violence in black communities and of the hard work

Pitjintjatjarra women were doing in their community to support victims and confront perpetrators. Back in Canberra we mounted a phone-in. So many stories. One is always with me. Again, as before, it involved a minister of religion.

'Hullo. I can't tell you my name. I live in Western Australia in a small country town. I'm married to a minister. He belts me but not where anyone can see the bruises. One day I plucked up the courage to go to the police. They laughed at me, told me I needed treatment. "Not the Reverend," they said, "he's a fine man." I went home and set up the tape recorder. I put it on to record just before he came home. He shouted abuse at me, hit me hard till I fell with a bump. I think my wrist was broken. After he had stopped and gone to his study, I cried. It was all recorded and next day when the children had gone to school I took the tape and lodged it at the bank with my will. When I am dead the children will know what happened.'

'Do you want someone to come and talk with you?'

'No, goodbye.'

In 1991 my father died. We had talked about so many things, feminism, pacifism, history, spirituality, but never enough. I miss him. When he got sick shortly before he died I was in the Women's Space tent at the World Council of Churches Assembly in Canberra. What luck to be with a great and supportive group of women at that time! I went up to Sydney to see Dad and drove back to Canberra joyfully anticipating the warm welcome and love I would get. It is a strange fact that when he died I did not feel overwhelming grief. That came later as I became more aware of what was no longer there for me.

My father was a quiet man and a deep thinker. He liked people and disliked small talk. He was no good at it. He loved his family, especially my mother whom he held in very high regard. Her craziness and foibles sometimes puzzled him but he realised what a wonderful foil they were to his seriousness.

'Ach Erika,' he would say, more in bemusement than in criticism, when she did or said something especially outrageous. When I think of Dad I see him as he looked in his later years, of average height and stocky build, strong white hair, big bushy eyebrows which he tugged when he was saying something thoughtful. He loved to walk and he loved the birds of the bush. My last walk with him was along the Shipley Plateau in the Blue Mountains. He was already experiencing pain in his legs, and walked very slowly.

'You'd better go back,' I said.

But he wouldn't. 'I like to walk with you, I'll go a little further.'

My last sabbatical, in the same year Dad died, involved travelling in the newly 'liberated' lands of Eastern Europe to meet with women and discover how they were coping with capitalism. In Poland I sat with a teacher and learned something of the great difficulties of adjusting to an individualist society. In Hungary I met a group of women who wanted to talk about domestic violence.

'The men are frustrated because they cannot get work and everywhere we are being told to buy the new goods. Instead they drink and bash their women. At least under the old regime we had women's committees that looked after these matters. Now we have to fight for everything. It is everyone for themselves.'

We travelled in Czechoslovakia, Poland, Hungary, Germany and the former Yugoslavia.

In Slovenia we met wonderful women who were working for peace. 'All the money goes for arms,' they said. 'As soon as we became an independent country our government stopped funding health and education and joined the arms race. We are trying to stop that.' I loved their spirit.

Two years later I left the university and together with Myra set up a house for people with intellectual disabilities. We did this for six, stretching years.

The work with these people, which I have written about elsewhere (see *Mira's Kitchen*), was another part of my peace journey. It is so easy to get irritated and then angry when dealing on a daily basis with people from whom you often expect more than they can give. I had worked for a while with handicapped children when I was 19 years old. My teacher told us that we should find out what our pupils could do and work with that.

'Everyone has a gift,' my teacher, Kyra Pohl, would say. 'We must find it and develop it – that is our task.' I tried to remember that when I was working with these adults, some of whom had been badly damaged by mistreatment at home or in institutions. Their gifts were often well hidden and it was a great challenge to find them. I also remember a conversation I had as a young teenager with my father.

'But he's stupid Dad. I can't get any sense out of him.'

'It is we who are stupid if we cannot find that of the spirit in him.'

I was not impressed at the time. 'Some people keep their spirit too well hidden,' I replied, thinking that he was too serious. But now I often remember his words and his love with gratitude.

Quakers have always been involved in prison work. Since the 17th century they have visited, agitated for prison reform, provided comforts and of course spent time in prison themselves for a variety of actions against injustice and war. I was impressed as a child to meet people who had been to prison as conscientious objectors. I thought they were so brave and I almost wished I had been born a man so I could refuse to go to war.

Two years ago I walked into Lithgow jail as part of a project called Alternatives to Violence (AVP). We passed through five locked gates and walked across a quadrangle before we reached the education centre where we were to meet the inmates. They were all dressed in green but they found ways to express their individuality despite being in that most conformist of all institutions. Some wore caps, some didn't, some had shorts on, some had removed the sleeves of their sloppies. Somehow they all managed to look different.

I had heard about AVP over the years and had thought about doing the training. I was a little wary because I had always been critical of programmes for violent offenders, men who bashed their wives. I believed that they only enrolled in courses to get their wives back and then the violence started all over again. I had heard so many stories. Could I work in a jail with violent men?

Laurel Thomas, a Friend whom I respected, worked in a local jail and talked to me about it. She was getting tired and was looking for someone else to take over some of the work. I agreed to do a course with her in the jail.

'It's about finding our creative, rather than our destructive, power. It's called transforming power,' she said. I was excited. It seemed to relate to all the things I'd been doing and thinking about, although it's far more practical than anything I was used to. I've always believed I was not a very practical person, and it's a new learning. However, I expect the best.

The programme is a voluntary one for both facilitators and participants and relies on experiential learning. Transforming power, at the heart of the programme, encompasses caring for others, expecting the best, looking for non-violent solutions, thinking before reacting and respecting oneself. Easy to say but not so easy to impart or to live out oneself!

I was nervous at first but found that on the whole long-serving inmates were looking for a different way to live their lives, and so were receptive and reasonably enthusiastic.

'When I get out I am going to live with my missus and the children near the river,' one chap said to me.

'How long will that be?'

'Only another 11 years,' he replied.

The inmates build a life in jail, especially if they are long-term prisoners. Our programme can be seen as an interruption, or a welcome break, depending on the person.

'You know miss,' one chap said to me after my second workshop, 'for these three days it was like I wasn't in prison.'

On the other hand when I asked a group of youthful offenders what they had learned from the three day programme, one replied, 'Nothing, miss, it's a waste of time.' He was a short-term inmate, looking forward to a life of ease with both beer and women on tap.

We play games, have fun, and look at different ways of communicating, listening and building an ideal community.

I do not see my role as agitating for prison reform like many of the early Quakers did but I am diminished by the lack of humanity displayed from time to time in these institutions. The small amount of power that these underpaid officers have is sometimes abused at the expense of inmates.

'My mum said she would send me some new jocks and socks,' one inmate told me. 'When I asked about them the officer said the rules had changed and I couldn't have them.' He went on to say that before doing AVP he would have ripped into this officer, with the result that he would have been locked in his cell for three days. Instead he decided to take it up with a prisoner's representative on the liaison committee. He did get his parcel.

The huge 19th century stone prison at Bathurst is at the initial encounter almost like revisiting Victor Hugo's *Les Miserables.* Usually we work in pairs at least, but I arrive for my first visit there on my own. The mighty wooden doors are locked tight. I press the bell, I am apprehensive; nobody comes. Eventually I knock on the wooden doors. My knock sounds feeble against the enormous timbers, but at last an officer opens a small door inside the larger doors. I come into a large, draughty entrance space. It has stone floors, is very cold, and has another set of gates at the end. Once I have signed in I am conducted through four more sets of locked gates to the X-wing where I will take my first Bathurst programme. My bag has been searched, no phones, food, or other bits and pieces are allowed. Prisoners might misuse anything, they have even been known to use sharpened toothbrushes to stab other inmates.

'I have checked with the Governor,' my guide tells me. 'You will be allowed to bring biscuits and cake on the last day of the course.' This treat is eagerly awaited by the inmates. 'When do we get the cake, Miss?' is their constant refrain. I am confronted, by the prison culture, the anger, the lack of self-esteem, the incredible feeling of violence, the yearning for family, the sexism, homophobia, and the bravado.

'I'm not violent,' one chap says, angrily. 'I don't know why I'm here.'

It's always a struggle but little things can let you end on a high. We have sometimes finished with a silent circle and I can feel a new strength coming from the inmates and myself. At the end of one Basic Course one of my most troublesome participants who had kept saying, 'I don't want to do this, it's silly,' and using his right to pass over and over said, 'When are you doing the Advanced? Can I do it? When? How soon Miss?'

Despite all the positives, the hardest thing for me, perhaps because of my so different father and my years of feminism, is the hatred of women which often exists in these men. They make plenty of statements about wonderful mothers and grandmothers who have stood by them, but other women are discussed as though they were dirt, mere belongings that need disciplining. It is as though their mothers, grandmothers or daughters are a breed apart, not to be compared with women generally. Many see women as responsible for all the ills of society, to be blamed for their situation or deserving of punishment for perceived transgressions. It is so hard for them to imagine themselves in a woman's shoes, although we do try through role-plays. It is as though we were another species. I have not really worked out a way of tackling this. Last time I was working with the young men who swear a lot and use 'cunt' constantly, I told them what a cunt was and asked them not to use it any more while I was around.

'OK,' one guy said, turning to his mate, 'You stupid penis.' We all laughed.

Often there is a lot of laughter as we play games to energise ourselves. Mrs Mumbly is a favourite. At first they think it's stupid but gradually we are all laughing together as we try to pass a message around the circle without showing our teeth. Another favourite is 'Jailbreak', a form of musical chairs. The inmates have many private jokes. 'Red rum' one said, and they all fell about laughing. It's 'murder' backwards I discovered later. They talk fairly disparagingly about the prison officers, with few exceptions. I suppose they need an enemy and sometimes it's hard to keep in my head the fact that these men and women officers are people of the spirit as well. It must often be a scary job, and fear can so easily turn to violence if no other alternatives are available.

Sometimes I have a conversation with myself about my doings, especially in the nights and very early mornings when I cannot sleep. It might go like this:

'Why are you doing this? Why do you march in protest against the war in Iraq?'

'I don't really know.'

'Is it to earn some kind of praise, a place in heaven perhaps?'

‘I don’t think so, anyway praise embarrasses me and I’m not sure if I believe in that sort of heaven, filled with goody-goodies.’

‘Well, what sort of heaven do you believe in?’

‘Perhaps a place where there isn’t violence.’

‘That sounds a bit idealistic, doesn’t it?’

‘I suppose so, but I think that’s one of the reasons I do this stuff, that I don’t like violence.’

‘Are there any other reasons you can think of?’

‘Well, we survived the holocaust, and I think that means we have a special responsibility, and there’s my Jewish heritage, and the influence of my parents, and my luck.’

‘What do you mean, your luck?’

‘Well, I just think I’ve been so lucky in my life – my family, my partner, my opportunities, lots of laughter and love. If you can laugh with people it’s easier to see their humanity and harder to see them as enemies.’

Sabine Erika

thoughts on war

. . . it's not a war, it's an invasion.
an evasion of responsibility.

a shrieking, piercing, shattering
quiet
a lull, where numbness
overtakes the predictability of daily life
the heart is drowning
in pain and anguish.

despair is not a word
in the vocabulary
of suited men,
men more suited to
lofty decisions in lofty towers
where
no fringe of humanity can
brush against worsted threads.

terror brings its uninvited presence
to the minds of the fearful
desperation cloaks the bodies of many
who have all but given up hope.

we
all
wait,

for this is not a war of
triumph and defeat

it is the savage
quiet before a storm.

helena wong
10 march, 2003

Fragments Of Memories: From Days In Latvia, Also Known as Dwinsk and Daugavpils, And from Days in South Africa

From the Days in Latvia

I wish that I had been more interested when my parents talked about their young lives in Latvia and Lithuania. Now there is no one to ask, as they have both died, and their siblings have died.

When we were all living in Germiston, in South Africa, I used to visit my parents with my children, and they loved seeing their grandparents Boba Rachel and Zaida Harry. We would sit together having a cup of tea and eating my mother's famous ginger biscuits, while she spoke about her life in the small village near Riga, in Latvia.

I remember snatches of what she said.

In her family there were ~~four~~ three sisters, my mother, Rachel, Bessie, and Feiga (Fanny) and four brothers, Nechemniah (who was the eldest child), Orkie, Phivas and Leslie.

She talked of the effects of the Revolution in Russia in 1917:

'Our money became worthless, you could paper the walls with it.'

And about the pain of being hungry:

'All we had some nights were potato peelings which we cooked up to make soup. My sisters and I would go to the Baltic Sea, which led into the Gulf of Riga, when we heard that the sprats had come in. We scooped the sprats into the skirts of our dresses and took them home for a feast.'

She told us how she had to trudge miles to school in the snow:

'I had to go every day. I couldn't let Bessie down because she had decided to make me the family scholar. She persuaded our parents, Tata and Ma, to let one of the younger children study and she chose me. She made me a uniform from a sheet she had dyed brown. I was so proud.'

My mother spoke a lot about her oldest sister Bessie. One story I remember tells how she saved the life of her friend Smuel (Samuel) It seemed far fetched to me, it was so far removed from our family life in South Africa.

Aunt Bessie's Story, as told by my Mother:

After the Revolution, most people dabbled on the black market to survive. Our cousins the Suckermans also lived in the village and they all took these risks. Our mother Chava, your boba, was always nervous about it.

Bessie was a strikingly beautiful young woman with long black hair, deep blue eyes and a slender graceful build. It wasn't surprising that cousin Abe Suckerman was smitten by her and eventually married her.

One day I was at school and Faiga and Leslie were in the fields tending the vegetables. Nechemniah was at the blacksmith's forge where he worked and Orkie and Phivas were out learning to be tailors.

Suddenly Bessie came into our house very distressed. 'Ma, Smuel has been taken to jail, he was arrested for selling on the black market. I have to help him.'

'Meine Kind, be careful,' Chava said.

'Ma, I need a bottle of the wine Nechemniah made for Pesach (Passover) and could I have the Chala you baked today?' (Chala was the Sabbath loaf of plaited bread.)

Chava nodded yes to both requests and, wringing her hands in fear, watched her daughter getting ready.

Bessie quickly found a sturdy basket, took a cloth from the linen shelf, went into her bed alcove, and fished out a trunk from under her bed. It held shoes and boots. She took out a strong pair of boots that Phivas had outgrown. Then she chose a peasant blouse and a full skirt from her clothing shelf, and put them on over the clothes she was wearing. She found two pretty scarves. Finally she grabbed her coat and cape and put them on as well.

She went to the medicine chest in the kitchen and took out the bottle of sleeping draught that Chava used when Zelig was in Africa and she couldn't sleep. She put some in the wine, and packed the basket carefully. She put one of the scarves on the bottom of the basket, put the boots on top, placed the cloth over that, then the wine and the bread and found a colourful tablecloth to cover it all. She put the scarf on her head, kissed Chava goodbye and left for the jail. As she walked she prayed to Hashem (God) to help Smuel.

'Hello Mr Slotnik,' she said respectfully, batting her eyelashes, and then looking at him with her gorgeous eyes. 'Could I please give Smuel a bit of bread? The rest is for you and your friend, and I have also brought you some delicious wine.'

He opened the cell and returned to his card game, first pouring two glasses of wine. It wasn't long before he and his companion were asleep. Bessie quickly took off her extra clothes and gave them to Smuel to wear. The boots fortunately fitted quite well. He placed the scarf on his head and presented as a pretty girl.

Bessie packed Smuel's old clothes in her basket under the cloths, and they left the jail. They sauntered down the road without being noticed, two girls out for a stroll.

Smuel left immediately for another village, and Bessie left for a holiday with a friend, reassuring herself that Mr Slotnik would be too ashamed to explain to the visiting magistrate that he'd had a prisoner and then lost him. And she was right.

From the Days in South Africa

In 1922 my mother's family, the Silvers, came to South Africa on a ship with their cousins, the Suckermans. They disembarked at Cape Town, took the train from there to Johannesburg, in the province of Transvaal, and went by horse and carriage to Germiston, a small town about 20 miles from Johannesburg.

My mother was then eighteen years old, and had met Edie on the journey to the new country. Edie was seventeen years old, and they became life long friends. So I knew her as Auntie Edie although she was no relation.

Auntie Edie:

Auntie Edie was short like my mum, probably only 4ft 10in, with red hair and creamy white skin, and green eyes. She married an older man who died of tuberculosis and so she had to bring up her two children, Janet and Morrie, on her own. She supported them by being an excellent seamstress. They lived in Johannesburg, and we spent many weekends together visiting each other.

I was very fond of her children. Morrie was the handsomest boy I had ever seen, with blond hair and blue eyes. I had a big crush on him. Janet wasn't as beautiful, but she made a deep impression on me because she was calm and wise. She had her mother's colouring, but she was a lot taller.

What I remember of Auntie Edie was her turned-down mouth and acid tongue. She constantly found fault with my father and thoroughly dominated my mother. 'Rachel,' she would say, 'do it like this.' All my home-made dresses looked home-made so my mum didn't listen too well.

One story about Auntie Edie that I will never forget happened long before I knew her. Dad took great delight in repeating the tale every chance he got.

My older brother Simon had just been born in the Florence Nightingale Hospital in Johannesburg. All the children in our family were born there including my four children. Dad's mode of transport was a motor- bike. He picked up Auntie Edie from her home to take her to the hospital to see mum and Simon. Probably Auntie Edie didn't hold onto dad tightly enough, because after a while he became aware that she was no longer behind him. He finally found her covered in mud with her silk stockings torn to shreds.

'You did it on purpose Harry,' she screamed at him.

When I was an adult I picked up on the fact that mum, using Auntie Edie as her confidante, vented too much to her, causing her to find fault with him. As a child I must have overheard much of this, and this coloured my attitude to my father, and to men in general.

I was born in the Florence Nightingale Hospital on the 6th December 1935, and the day after that my cousin Eleanor was born there too. Uncle Orkie and Auntie Rae, her parents, were kind to me and I spent a great deal of time at their home. Staying there I had my first taste of luxury, order and fine living.

Auntie Rae:

Their house was in Cachet Road Germiston. It was on an acre of land. The front garden had a large circular drive, terraced flower-beds and a large fish-pond in the middle of the lawn. In the pond, there were big goldfish and a fountain in the form of a statue of a girl holding a jug, from which the water cascaded into the pond.

They had a Great Dane dog, called Boy, who terrified me at first, but when I got to know him and his gentle nature I grew to love him.

It was a huge contrast to our life-style. I was one of five children, but Ele (Eleanor) had only one sibling, a brother named Natie, the same age as my brother Simon. We had a black maid called Maggie, but Auntie Rae's servants were a coloured lady called Ada, who was almost white skinned, and a black man-servant called Elijah, who doubled as the butler. I was so impressed when he served us our dinner, dressed in a white suit and gloves, with a red sash worn at an angle from one shoulder, and tied at his waist.

When I stayed with them I discovered that I liked olives as well as lollies, and I'm afraid their stores of both were depleted as I raided the fridge and the silver sweet dish whenever I couldn't sleep.

My best experience was when the family took me on holiday with them to the Empress Hotel in Durban, in the Province of Natal. Durban was at the seaside and the Empress was a luxury hotel on the Esplanade. The hotel was just beautiful. It was calm and smoothly run, and the food was well prepared and presented with great style. I loved the ambience, especially dressing up for dinner. I think I got my taste for the finer things in life from these days with my relatives.

I was fourteen on this holiday, and I was asked out on my first date. Of course I was very excited and Auntie Rae set my hair for me and combed it out in a flattering style. I wore an olive green taffeta, black polka-dotted dress. How generous she was! Ele wasn't going out that night and I really appreciated her going to so much trouble for me.

Those times were important to me, as I didn't relate to my life at home, where my dad always dreamed of striking it rich, trying new adventures and schemes that didn't work. He actually was on the verge of bankruptcy when a miracle happened. Dad and a friend had taken a risk and shared a lottery ticket, in the Irish Sweep. Sweepstakes were illegal in Calvinistic South Africa, but they had the winning ticket, and the excitement was extreme. I have a memory of the open safe in my parents' bedroom, with papers and tickets spilling out all over the floor. Dad was looking for the winning ticket, which he finally found. My mother was convinced it was her prayers that had been answered, but we all agreed it was dad's luck, as he won a second time, in the Malta Sweep eight years later.

Our lives were filled with barmitzvahs, births, deaths and weddings. The barmitzvahs and weddings were held in our beautiful Synagogue.

It was an old-fashioned building with marvellous stained glass windows. The sun would stream in and I would really feel that I was in a holy place whenever I was there. The women were seated upstairs and the men downstairs. The Bimah (platform), where the Rabbi, the Chazen (Choir-master), the barmitzvah boys, and honoured male congregants stood, was made of carved mahogany wood.

The Holy Scrolls were housed in the Ark, which faced the Bimah. Blue velvet curtains embroidered in white silk thread hung in front of the ark, and when the curtains were opened we all stood in reverence. Above the Ark was the eternal flame, protected in an ornate light fitting. There was also a Chuppa (Canopy) in front of the Ark, held up by four tall posts. When couples enter this space to be married it is symbolic of being in God's presence, and the couple's first home together. At the end of the ceremony the groom shatters a cloth-covered glass goblet with a hearty thump of his shoe, and all the congregation joyously calls out: 'Mazeltov' (Good luck).

I remember one family wedding in particular, not because of the ceremony, but because of a family scandal.

Auntie Bessie:

Auntie Bessie had married her cousin Abe Suckerman after the families moved to Germiston. They had four children and I was close to all of them. But a sad thing happened. Auntie Bessie had a bad stroke, and it was only with a great deal of hard work with nurses, speech therapists and physiotherapists that she learned to walk with a stick, and was able to talk again in a way that could be understood.

Now at this wedding, the dinner had been eaten, and the speeches were over. The band had finished the Bridal Waltz, and everyone was invited to get up and dance.

I was thrilled to be asked to dance by one of the friends of my brother Simon. I was fifteen years old and it was the year of the 'New Look', which was a fashion that was flattering to me. My outfit was green crepe trimmed with a tartan taffeta waistband and cuffed sleeves in the same trim. The skirt was a calf-length flared style, that twirled as I danced. I felt svelte and sophisticated in it.

As we danced past Auntie Bessie's table I saw her getting out of her chair and whacking Uncle Abe on his back with her walking stick yelling: 'Bastard!' He had danced boldly past her holding his mistress, Lily, tightly in his arms. People were surprised, many secretly applauding Auntie Bessie's courage. Everyone knew about the affair, but I felt he could have been more discreet and not caused his wife such humiliation.

I had so much admiration for Auntie Bessie, especially because of how hard she tried to become strong again after her stroke. At that time I hadn't yet learned of her beauty and bravery in her youth.

Mira Sonik

each moment

the glass beside me is empty
i sit,
still,
in the light
of early evening.
it is as if every moment of this day
and every hour
of every other day of my life
is compressed
into an instant.

if i were to turn my head
and look out the open
window
only dust on the sill
would tell me
time existed
before now.

i pause,
the news of my sister's death
before me.
the television hums,
mute
as pictures flash flickers of light
across the screen.

every fear that
ever haunted me
cowers
behind that nameless chill,
the coldness that starts
in my toes, works its way up
through the body
and leaves me, hand outstretched,
reaching for the glass.

reaching out, watching in
to find the precious gem
that stores the memory of her breath,
our life together.

helena wong
16 may, 2003

Vespina

I don't know how many times, driving along the awkward bit of dogleg highway that crosses the railway line at Medlow Bath, I have quickly turned my head and had the same thought. Heading east, as I come around the bend, I have to crane my neck to see if she is there, the solitary woman in the hamburger shop. It's the only shop in sight, and she is always there, mostly alone, in her blue, sometimes brown, zip-up uniform, and old worn cardigan.

My life is so full, busy, and often noisy. It takes me regularly up and down that highway, across that railway line, to and fro past that shop window to a multitude of activities and people. And there she is. A melancholy figure in a window.

I wonder what she thinks about, if she really is sad or lonely, or simply content. I do not comprehend what appears to be – a singular woman in a dimly lit shop, day after day, night after night.

She stands, with her arms often crossed and resting calmly, gazing out through the large glass shopfront window. From behind her counter, trance-like, she just stares … at the road, at the traffic, at the old brick railway station that divides the town.

At other times, she seems oblivious to the passing world, focused and head down, facing the stainless steel wall of ovens, cook tops, and deep fry hot oil that constantly spits away. She cleans and scrubs and wipes, and from my car I see her arm moving in circular motions, head bent, and alone. The shop is almost always empty, so I wonder what could possibly have produced the mess or dirt that requires the incessant scrubbing and tidying. And then she waits.

Trains wind up and down the mountain on their singular track, ceaselessly committed to their timetable, and to picking up and dropping off a myriad travellers. A never-ending stream of vehicles flows east to west, west to east, through the seasons, sun and rain, snow, fog and mist. I have seen the odd truckie pull over, and amble in for a burger and chips, a coke, or a packet of smokes. It's a difficult spot to park.

Her shop is perched on the edge of the cliff face that overlooks the Megalong Valley, and there is a sense of decay and neglect about the mustard coloured brick building, and the fibro house, tacked onto the side and back. Next door, a vacant block, with unmown grass and tumbling fence, spills over the escarpment.

'She must live there,' I think whenever I pass by, 'with a stunning view.' I note that it is the same view enjoyed by the neighbouring famous Hydro Majestic Hotel, where thousands of unsuspecting tourists pay an exorbitant price for a cup of coffee and a seat beside the expansive glass walls that hover above the valley.

I am tempted to go in, and find out more, but what would I say? How could I strike up a conversation without seeming intrusive?

Directly opposite on the other side of the line, is the only other shop in the village - a second-hand bookstore in the old local Post Office now owned by Stefan, the heavily accented Austrian I once met at the Saturday afternoon Katoomba marketplace. I will always cherish the book I bought from his stall, a real find called *One Special Summer*, joyfully written and illustrated in 1951 by Jacqueline and Lee Bouvier, teenage sisters embarking by ship on their first unaccompanied trip to Europe. The naïve and funny drawings by Jacqueline (later Jackie Kennedy) are a visual delight.

Maybe Stefan can shed some light on the enigmatic figure over the railway line.

The maroon timber weatherboard building feels cold and gloomy, and because it houses ten thousand books, he tells me he is not allowed to light the wood fuelled stove. He has, however, created a small café near the entrance, and proudly boasts about his homemade Viennese cooking, including 'schnitzel' and 'apfel' Strudel.

'I vill make you an excellent cup of free coffee,' he says, 'if you vont to sit and have a chat,' ushering me towards a table covered in synthetic lace over plastic.

Here is my opportunity.

We chat a little about books, and how business is slow, and consider the impact of his being on the 'wrong' side of the railway line. This of course brings me to the subject of the shop on the 'right' side of the line. 'Do you know the lady who works in there? How does *she* survive?'

'Vell, I don't know rilly much,' Stefan shrugs, 'but zat she owns ze business, and she has a son who has a motorbike, and a daughter who lives here in Medlow Bath. And zat is all.'

Dead end.

Days and weeks pass by, and so do I. Autumn leaves change the colour of the road, and the clouds move, changing formation, disguising the distant hills on the horizon. Mists roll in and out, but nothing changes in the unanimated shop on the highway.

Then one unchosen day, my curiosity wins, and drawn as if by magnet, my car comes to rest outside the entrance.

The brown metal screen door slams behind me as I enter the yellow-green fluorescence of the empty shop, and I wonder what I can buy, my eyes quickly scanning the space. I see sparsely filled shelves with an odd assortment of grocery items, and commercial wire racks displaying packets of chips and white sliced bread. Tall, brightly coloured soft drink fridges hum beside the faded walls, and a pile of daily newspapers rests on the laminated counter. I slowly circumnavigate the small laminex dining tables, and approach her across the weathered linoleum floor.

Finally we are face to face.

'Hello,' I smile.

She responds with a broad grin across her olive, worn face. Her shoulder length corrugated hair is parted to the side, its blackness interrupted by a multitude of grey strands.

'I'd like some mineral water, thank you.' I pay, then hesitate, and linger as I remove the lid and begin to drink from the plastic bottle.

'Mmm, I'm so thirsty, it's such a windy day. I suppose you'd get strong winds coming up from the valley too?'

'Yes, sometimes,' she replies, and shyly looks down.

The moment is awkward, but I can't leave now, with so little information.

‘My name’s Josephine, what’s yours?’

‘Valerie,’ she offers hesitantly, in a soft voice.

‘Oh, I detect an accent, are you Greek?’ I guess with eyebrows raised.

‘No,’ (cautiously) ‘I’m from Cyprus, an island near to there.’

‘Ah, then Valerie must be your Australian name.’ I smile, trying to make her feel more at ease.

‘Yes,’ she says, her eyes summing me up, ‘my real name is Vespina.’

‘Well, it was nice to meet you, Vespina. I’ll see you again,’ and as she silently smiles and nods, I make my way back to the car. I can’t question her any further without seeming too inquisitive.

My shopping trips to Katoomba, dance class in Wentworth Falls, yoga and friends in Leura, continue to ping-pong me past the woman in the shop window. But now she is Vespina. On another return trip home, I pull up behind a large freight truck, and venture in. I smell hamburger, and the lone truck driver is just finishing his meal, flicking over the pages of a newspaper.

This time I purchase milk, one always needs milk, and indulge myself with a perpetually self-denied packet of Twisties. The truckie pushes back his chair, tosses his serviette onto the plate, pays at the counter, and then to my horror replaces the used Telegraph on the pile of papers for sale, and leaves.

Vespina is not the type to make something of it. I feel indignant for her, then sad that she simply accepts this kind of behaviour as if she had no voice.

When she turns to the cash register, I notice a scald mark on the back of her cardigan, where she has come too close to the griller against the wall.

'Hello again, do you remember me from the other week?'

Vespina doesn't really remember, I can tell, but I persevere.

'Do you live here, out the back?'

'Mmm,' with a nod.

'You must have a wonderful view.'

'Mmm.'

'Have you been here long?'

I now sense a glimmer of recognition as Vespina cautiously opens up to me.

'Yes, twenty years ago I came with my husband. He came first to Australia. We had a café before in Cyprus. Then he came back to there to get me, and after, we bought here.'

'And you both worked here?'

'Mmm, but he became very sick and now I am alone.' She shrugs resignedly, tilting her head.

'Oh, I'm sorry. Do you have any family, or friends to keep you company?'

'I have two children, but not much friends.'

'But you must go out sometimes, it's good for you,' trying to lighten the mood.

'Mm…no,' she shrugs again, dismissively, 'I'm too old for that, too old for anything … I don't go anywhere.'

I am taken aback by her acquiescence, her defeatism. She would only be in her early sixties, I guess. Again I feel that I can continue no further.

'Well then, take care Vespina, I'll see you next time,' and I try to prevent the fly screen door from slamming shut behind me.

However, there is no next time.

For a short while I continue to see Vespina from my car, insular in her world. A world in slow motion as I pass by in a conveyor belt of traffic.

One afternoon shrouded in mist, she is not there. Startled, I slow down, stretch my neck for a better look, and notice the 'Closed' sign butted up against the front door, and then, even worse, large cracks in the glass shopfront window. At their centre is what looks like a perfectly round bullet hole and immediately I have fears for her safety.

Now I drive by with concern and worry, rather than fascination and curiosity, each time hoping to see the familiar scene I have come to expect. The next change is the pages of newspaper stuck together all over the shopfront, completely concealing the interior. Quite suddenly the mood is eerie, and I feel compelled by some strange attachment, to enquire after her at the house.

Warily I push open the rusty squeaky gate, follow the unruly path down the side of the building and knock on the door. No answer, so I venture towards the back, and look through the bare window into the kitchen, with its 1950's style painted timber cupboards and empty bench tops. It is devoid of any sign of life – except for a very large black motorbike parked in the centre of the room. Further along the corrugated ironclad extension I reach the laundry, the only room with a view. The backyard is overgrown, long grass clawing its way up the Hills Hoist.

I sit down amongst dandelions, the sun on my back, to contemplate. Before me a wondrous landscape unfolds as the yard dips steeply away through thick olive-green virgin bush down to the fertile cradle of the Megalong Valley. Deep blue and violet hues then draw my focus up to the distant hills silhouetted on the horizon. For years Vespina has roused from sleep beside this vista, then spent the long hours of a working day with her back turned to it.

Before too long the plate glass window has been repaired, and a 'To Let' sign replaces the 'Closed' one. I wait in anticipation.

At home in Mt Victoria the phone rings. 'Hello darling,' and I welcome the cheerful voice of my mother. 'Guess what, a lovely young woman from Medlow Bath just phoned and she plans to make a documentary about four inspiring women of different faiths who are giving back to the community. She has a Buddhist, a Muslim, a Christian, and she has chosen me as the Jew. I don't know how she heard about me, but she wants to film the human rights work I do with the schoolchildren.' Her enthusiasm is infectious.

'How exciting!' I agree. 'What a wonderful idea!'

'And because you live so close, it would probably be most interesting for you two to meet, and exchange ideas.'

A late summer's afternoon, and I am waiting in the cool of Mt Victoria's stone railway station to meet Rachel, the filmmaker. Instant rapport over the telephone has brought us together, and the feeling is mutual when a lively redhead hugs me warmly saying, 'It's so good to meet you.'

Back in my yellow dining room, the western sun streams through leadlight windows casting jewels of colour over the tablecloth, and we chat like old mates over tea and cake. Her energy is effusive as she talks with passion about women, and her film. It feels right then to confide in her that I too am working on a story about an intriguing woman who also lives in Medlow.

'Really… who?' she asks with interest.

'Well, you know the little take away hamburger …'

Her wide-eyed laugh stops me in my tracks. 'I don't believe it, you mean Val! She's my future mother-in-law!'

'What!'

We stare at each other frozen in disbelief.

'Where is she? What happened… the hole in the window?' Questions flow as I seek the answers to my wild imaginings.

'Uh… she had a stroke, but she's okay now.' Rachel recognises my concern, and hastily adds that she's recovering quite well, though she's walking slowly and doesn't speak English as well as she used to. 'A few days later some youths armed with slingshots, fired ball bearings at the window. They picked on shops along the highway in Katoomba as well, but the police finally caught them.'

'Hmm … I thought it was a bullet hole, I didn't know what to think.'

My relief turns to laughter as we muse over the bizarre coincidence that I am writing about her mother-in-law, while she is making a film about my mother.

I tingle at the thought that this serendipity is about to provide the missing pieces of my puzzle. Our meeting has taken on a new and more profound meaning, and we continue to talk about the two older women in our lives.

'What will happen now that she's had the stroke?'

'Well, she doesn't want to sell, although the hyenas sniff around the door. Too much of her life is tied up there. She's raised her family, and watched the local children grow up.'

'Tell me more … do you know her well?'

'Not really,' taking another sip of tea. 'She doesn't say much, but in her quiet way passes on words of sound advice, like "Be careful with your choices" and "Think about your future". I'd love to read your story … and I can't wait to tell Aristo. You'll meet him soon, he's coming to pick me up.'

Vespina's son seems a little apprehensive when we tell him our news. He has a serious and cautious demeanour, pausing in thought before he speaks. I sense his protectiveness towards his mother and do not push for answers, but try to explain my fascination with the image of the 'unknown woman', and how I came to fear for her safety, and visited the house to offer some help.

He relaxes the concerned furrow in his brow. 'You know, my Dad was very hard working too. Before they had the shop, he was employed at the Hydro, and even Caves House at Jenolan Caves.'

'Yes, Vespina must really miss him, they witnessed a lot of change together.'

'Mum misses the café too. Now there's very little to do but pass the time of day ... although she *has* started a small vegetable garden.'

'And the motorbike?' I have to know.

'Oh, that belongs to my sister, Maria,' as if it is hardly surprising. 'Mum lives with her now, over the railway line.'

The young couple prepare to leave. I want to tug and pull them back, for I cannot help but feel that I have only gained a small window of insight into Vespina's world. I am no closer to knowing her.

For months the shop remains empty. I even forget to look.

Then one westbound afternoon, I spot an open door and a sandwich board menu on the pavement outside. A breath of new life on the corner. Inside, the walls have been whitewashed, modern silver lampshades hang long from the ceiling, and there's a state-of-the-art espresso coffee machine gleaming on the counter beside a vase of fresh flowers. It looks promising.

The young new proprietor is cheerful, chatty and optimistic, but as weeks pass I do not share her optimism. The plan to widen the highway into a motorway has already begun at her doorstep.

'Oh, that doesn't worry me,' she says, straightening her back, chin held high.

'The road workers are keeping me in business wanting snacks, lunches and even dinners as they work into the night.'

More and more heavy machinery arrives. Tractors, cranes and bulldozers create noise and traffic delays in their determination to build the new overpass that will change this dogleg corner forever. Cement dust whirls around in the wind, and now huge concrete slabs split the highway.

Vespina's shop is hardly visible from the road. Access is difficult and there is nowhere to park. Eventually the doors are shut tight, and once again newspapers appear over the windows, yellowing in the sunlight. The bookstore has closed too.

Only once, I catch sight of a lone figure slowly following the road beside the railway line, hands clasped behind her. I recognise the wedge-shaped silhouette of her hair, and the cardigan. She pauses to catch breath, then ambles on closer to the overpass, stopping to stare at the hard-hat workers, and witness the inevitable.

I continue my journeys along this stretch of road. There are no alternative routes, and I learn patience, listening to music and waiting as the oncoming traffic takes its turn to edge forward.

I no longer crane my neck, but rather reflect on the worth of this other journey, one of discovery. Gone is the busy heyday of the café, but Vespina's days were not empty. They were warmed by contemplation and memory, her calm stillness completing a comforting paradox in a corner of the world where time to stop and take notice is brief.

Josephine Wolanski

Renovating Cairo

It was spring, the season of new beginnings. I alighted from the bus at the southern-most end of Bondi Beach and stood for a moment looking at the sunlight gently sparkling on the water. The warm air moving softly past my bare arms as I walked felt strange after the long winter. The trapped feeling that had been with me for so long shifted slightly and I felt a sense that there were possibilities after all. A roughly lettered sign advertised a flat to let. I looked at the building. All I could see was a tiled entrance flanked by shops and a Malaysian restaurant. A weathered awning prevented any closer acquaintance. I crossed the road for a better view. It was a long, squat building, with two floors of flats above the shops. Its shabby condition belied its name, spelt out in proud capitals: CAIRO MANSIONS. I found its shabbiness encouraging. It seemed to say 'You could afford to live here. Yes, even you.'

'Enquire at 110 Campbell Parade' the sign suggested. A block down the road I found Number 110, a seedy boarding house called The Biltmore Hotel. I climbed the stairs and made my way down a dark and narrow corridor which smelled like all boarding house corridors with their layered traces of mundane history: unwholesome meals and unaired space, unwashed laundry and unsurprised disappointment. One room had its door open and a weak shaft of natural light fell onto the hallway carpet.

I hovered outside for a moment, hesitant to actually peer in. A modest orange beehive appeared around the door, soon followed by the rest: a short stout personage dressed in leopard skin print and stilettos, a look both behind and ahead of its time in the spring of I982.

'Hello, dear, can I help you?' She had sharp, quick eyes, like a bird's.

'I'm interested in the flat to let.'

'Yes, dear, it's got two bedrooms and it's $90 a week.'

'Could I have a look at it?'

'Yes, dear, I'll just find the key.'

She lifted the flap of a handmade storage cabinet on her desk to reveal a mysterious but orderly arrangement of hooks and keys. The whole room was a triumph of order in the face of a ludicrous disparity between space and matter. A single bed, a bar fridge, the desk, a wardrobe and sundry clutter in the area of a child's bedroom. The desk was storage space rather than work area. Where does she eat? I wondered.

'Here it is.' She held up the key like a trophy. 'Do you want a deposit?' I asked.

'No, dear, you've got an honest face. You'll be back.' She smiled in a thin straight line. What other knowledge was held with such certainty under that copper beehive?

I was glad I could look at the flat by myself. In my limited experience as a prospective tenant, I'd found it difficult to get a feeling for a place with an anxious and hurried agent at my elbow. The flat was large by Bondi standards. It was on the top floor. A hallway ran along the back, connecting the larger bedroom with the bathroom and giving onto the other bedroom and living area. The kitchen was minute, just a timber frame separating a sink, stove and narrow shelves from the living area. It was kind of cute, I decided, like a doll's house. All three rooms had a view of the beach. This was a very impressive feature in a Bondi flat. Usually, the views were so sparingly apportioned that many flats were long and thin, with each room opening into the next until you reached the last room which boasted 'the view.' The flat faced east and was full of light. It was perfect, except for the wallpaper and floor coverings, but I could fix that. I'd pull up the aged carpet and lino, and slap around a bit of white paint. When I found myself using the toilet, I knew it was mine. The primitive within was marking its territory. I returned to the Biltmore.

'Is there a bond?'

'Oh, yes, dear. Two weeks bond and two weeks rent in advance. $360.' $360. My heart sank as reality intruded. But I made arrangements to be back the following day with feigned confidence.

Three hundred and sixty dollars, I mused on the bus. Three hundred and sixty dollars. It wasn't really that much money. I must be able to raise it somehow. I would have to do my planning in transit. Once I got back to Lane Cove, hopelessness would reclaim me. Mum and Dad wouldn't help out with relocation; that had been established finally. I had spent weeks steeling myself to ask Dad to help me set myself up and start again, but day after day, my courage failed me. Sometimes I'd sit there in the lounge room till he got up to go to bed, still hoping I could bring myself to ask him. The reason I was so afraid to ask him was the desolation I anticipated if he said no.

So long as I didn't ask, it was still a possibility. If he said no, the only door I could find in my dungeon would prove to be locked against me.

Over and over I asked myself why I had gone back. But I'd had no choice in the end, the end of my first failed attempt at adult life. As soon as things had started to fall apart, people had suggested a strategic retreat to the family home to rebuild my strength. They assumed the family home was a place of nurture. 'Your mother knows you better than anyone,' Elisabeth said. They almost convinced me, but deep down I knew how it would be, and I resisted until I had nowhere else to go. So there I was, 23 and already a failure at life, dependent again on my parents for my basic needs, dependent on them to help me make a new start.

But when I finally asked Dad, he said no. He said I could stay with them, get a job and save the money myself. How could they understand that it took all my energy to endure being there? When I imagined moving between an office and their house, with no space of my own in which to reclaim myself, the thought of it exhausted me. I was so sure they wouldn't understand that I didn't even try to explain it to them. I slipped into new depths of hopelessness. Maybe I would sit there till I was 45, still trying to deal with my demons in their own breeding ground. More likely I would never manage it, not there. I needed distance, space, privacy, freedom. I needed fresh air. The atmosphere of my parents' house oppressed me totally, daily defeated me. Some days it was a triumph to get out of my nightie. It was hard to see the point, when I'd only have to put it on again to go to bed.

Sometimes I'd watch an absorbing midday movie and for a while forget the black cloud I was living in. I'd be flying down to Rio with Fred and Ginger, or resolving a Kubrick moral dilemma, or putting on the show that would save the whole town, or finally discovering who'd committed the murder. The moment it was over, my troubles would press down on me again, but the fact that they could be forgotten, however briefly, made them seem less substantial.

I avoided Mum and Dad. I'd stay up late after they went to bed, which enabled me to avoid their company in the mornings as well. If I was awake, I'd stay downstairs in my room till I heard them leave. Then I'd shower and change, if I could be bothered, and mess around all day, reading or watching TV. Sometimes I'd ask Mum for some money to go and see a friend, hoping it would make me feel better. I could skate around what was happening to me and enjoy something in the immediate present, a movie, fish and chips on the beach or a walk in beautiful surroundings, I would come back feeling better, affirmed in my precarious sense of self. But if I saw a baffled look, or if the friend asked me about things and couldn't understand my answers or the attitudes behind them, then I came back feeling utterly isolated. Even my friends didn't understand me. But then neither did I. So I'd return to Lane Cove and the daily struggle with phantoms.

Anyway, Dad had said no and that was that. He was not a man given to changing his mind. The 380 bus dropped me at Martin Place and I walked down Martin Place to Wynyard. It was afternoon now, and the sun only cleared those concrete cliffs to shine into the city streets at lunch-time. I shivered, folded my arms and wished I'd thought to bring a jumper. Soon I was sitting on the Lane Cove bus, up the back where the seat was warmed by the engine. As the bus crossed the Harbour Bridge, and I gazed out at the slow movement of boats on the tranquilly glittering harbour, my mind soon returned to my dilemma.

So, where else could I get the $360? I briefly considered asking friends but no, it would be too embarrassing. Even splitting it between three or four of them, it was a lot to ask for as a loan, and the chance of embarrassment was multiplied by three or four. No. I was really only left with Mr Jarman, my bank manager, one of the cabin crew of my recently derailed adult life. When I had moved into my first flat at Bondi, I'd gone to my local branch to convert my school passbook account to a grown up account. The holder still contained a little cardboard folder where koala, kangaroo and possum stamps rewarded each deposit. Mr Jarman was an older man with a large family, mostly young adults like me, and he liked me. He was worth a try.

I hurried down the leafy streets between the bus stop on the Pacific Highway and the deceptively comfortable calm of that road I had flown up so many times, hair streaming, schoolbag bumping, to catch the 266. I looked at my watch. Five past four. Perfect. The bank would be closed, and Mr Jarman would be in a good mood to take my call. I unlocked the door and went straight to the phone, before I could lose my nerve. I didn't shut the door behind me, but turned my back to the house and all it had come to represent, and stood at the hall phone looking out the front door at the impatiens.

'Miss Gentle,' boomed his jovial, avuncular voice. 'I haven't heard from you for a while. What have you been doing with yourself?'

What indeed? 'I've been staying at Mum and Dad's for a while.'

'Oh, that's nice. What can I do for you?'

'Well, I was over in Bondi today and I saw this really good flat. It's a cheap rent, so it'll be gone soon. But it would cost me $360 to move in. I could wait months for another one to come up as good as this. And I can get work over that side, so I was wondering …'

'Your parents can't help you out?'

'No, they - no.'

'Could you get yourself over here tomorrow morning, say ... 10.30?'

'Yes.'

'All right. Come in then and we'll see what we can do.'

When I walked out of the bank the next morning I had $360 in my hand. Mr Jannan, my new favourite person in the world, had given me an overdraft on my cheque account. Five minutes later, I was back at the Biltmore as promised.

'Hello, dear, you're back then. I thought you'd be back.' She made out two receipts, one for the bond and one for the rent in advance. When she took my name, she volunteered hers. Mrs Crate. 'Just think of a crate of beer and you'll think of me.' I could see her as the perfect barmaid, all good humour on the surface but quite unyielding underneath.

Ten minutes after I had left the bank I was walking up to my new flat, light on my feet, swinging my arms and singing: 'What a Difference a Day Makes.' I paced around the flat in great excitement, planning how I would pull up the carpet, strip the wallpaper and paint the walls. It already had basic furniture, a double bed in one room and a single in the other, a wardrobe, a couple of garden benches and a huge old wooden table. I went down to my new local milk bar and bought a sandwich which I took back to the flat. I sat at the window, eating my sandwich and drinking in the view. Two or three hours went by as I did nothing but revel in the freedom of my own space, freedom from the sense of surveillance, the apprehensive monitoring of my every move and facial expression, the consciousness that even the traces of my activity in my parents' absence were being surveyed for clues, clues to what had happened to what was generally considered my Early Promise.

'I don't know what went wrong,' said Dad on one of the rare occasions when my unnamed condition was openly referred to.

'You had a good brain.'

'Brains aren't all there is,' I said.

He looked surprised. 'Well, whatever else there is, it runs a poor second,' he said with finality.

Mum gave me a memory test. She said it was for her university studies, but I had my doubts. I did it anyway. My life was so barren that a memory test seemed almost like fun. She read a list of unrelated words at predetermined intervals, using a stopwatch. I spun an unlikely narrative in my head, marking the key words with an imaginary fluorescent highlighter pen.

When Mum turned off the stop-watch and held her pen poised for ticking, I silently recalled the story and reeled off most of the words in order. Mum looked puzzled. 'But that's better than anyone in my tute group got' she said, looking at me sideways but searchingly. Apparently the crashed daughter still had a good brain. So the mystery deepened and the surveillance continued.

My eyes again focused on the intense blue of the sea. I stretched and walked around the rooms again. In every room, I stretched my arms out like wings. I felt myself uncurling, un-hunching, expanding. As the shadow of Cairo Mansions crept over the park opposite, I prepared myself for the final scene of my sojourn at Lane Cove. I took a fast look around and locked the door behind me. I kept the key in my hand. When it became moist, I let it warm the other hand. Its sharp edges reminded me that this trip was only a visit. Just picking up my things. There weren't many of them.

I told them at dinner. 'Where did you get the money?' they wanted to know.

'I got an overdraft.'

They exchanged a glance which expressed incredulity at such irresponsible lending practices. But they didn't seem terribly sorry to see me go. Who could blame them? I hadn't been what you'd call good company. And my presence required awkward explanations when the few visitors they had called around. There was no sorrow, but there was bafflement. They still didn't understand what had happened and now the chapter was ending without resolution. It wasn't how it should have been. Maybe, if I had regained my health under their care and had been waved off fresh-cheeked and smiling, repaired and roadworthy, they could have felt good about the whole episode. As it was, I was as sullen and sulky as I'd ever been and all they could do was shrug and say I could borrow the car to take my things over.

There wasn't much to take, just a few cardboard boxes, mostly clothes and books. I was glad. I didn't want my new beginning hampered by the detritus of the past. Unpacking was easy. I put the clothes in the wardrobe, bedclothes on the bed and left the books in the boxes. I put a few things around, toiletries in the bathroom, hairbrush and make-up in the bedroom. When I got back with the car, Mum and Dad weren't home, so I left the key on the table and walked up to the bus stop to start the journey home.

The night I finished pulling up the carpet, I went out for a late meal. I had become so involved in the task and so focused on completing it that I'd gone beyond hunger twice. Now it was after ten o'clock and I was ravenous. There had been layers of carpet. Apparently none had ever been removed. New carpet was just laid over the old, sometimes without even vacuuming first. I found buttons, bobby pins and a lot of dust on my way down to the floorboards. Now the last gritty roll had been dragged down to the footpath and after a quick shower, I was ready to eat.

I walked down Campbell Parade, wondering what would still be open. Papa Giovanni's would be. I mentally surveyed their menu and was ready to order cannelloni before I reached the restaurant door. As I entered, the boys were in good humour. I ordered the cannelloni. Tony gestured towards the opening in the back wall through which the meals were passed from the kitchen to the restaurant. A small man with curly brown hair was looking through, surveying the restaurant.

'This is Romolo,' said Tony. 'He is new. He is not long in Australia. His English is not so good.' He spoke to Romolo in Italian. Romolo replied with a short Italian phrase and a grin that transformed his face from unremarkable to handsome.

'Ciao,' I said to Romolo, and to Tony, 'I've always wanted to learn Italian.'

'Romolo can teach you, and you can teach him English.'

Romolo's smile vanished as he struggled to understand this statement which contained his name. 'Teach me something,' I said to Tony.

'Io cerco imperare di parla Italiano.'

'What's that?'

'I want to learn to speak Italian.'

'Io cerco...'

'Io cerco imperare...' he prompted patiently.

'Io cerco imperare...'

'Io cerco imperare di parla Italiano.'

'Io cerco imperare parla Italiano.'

'Io cerco imperare *di* parla Italiano.'

'lo cerco imperare di parla Italiano.'

'Bene.'

The last group of diners had left and I was the only customer left in the restaurant. All the workers who'd been lounging around listening, cheered my triumph.

'I teach you something else,' said Tony. 'Io cerco imperare...'

'Io cerco imperare di chiavarde.'

'Io cerco imperare di chiavarde.'

The boys exploded in laughter. When they saw my puzzled face, they only laughed more. Romolo was wiping his eyes. I realised I'd been tricked, but decided to be a good sport. 'Don't tell me what I said.'

Tony shook his head solemnly, implying that he would never say such a thing in the presence of a lady. He brought me my cannelloni and turned over the sign in the window so that it said 'Open' to us, but 'Closed' to everyone outside. The boys started to clean up the restaurant. As they finished, Tony poured them a drink. As he passed my table, he poured me a drink too. It was wine, a bit sour, but not unpleasant. When I'd finished eating, I made to leave. Tony held up his hands to discourage me and poured me another drink. When they'd finished cleaning up, Tony asked me if I wanted to come back to his flat for a joint. I hesitated. A joint would be nice, but I hardly knew Tony. 'We all go there,' he said. For some reason, that reassured me and we went: me, Tony, Romolo, and another waiter.

When we arrived, two other men were waiting for the wage-earners and their grass to arrive. They wasted no time and a water-pipe was soon circulating. Romolo sat next to me and we made small talk in broken English. I tried to tell him a story I'd heard on the news. 'A woman found a snake,' – I gestured and hissed – 'in her baby's cot.' – I mimed rocking a baby and putting it in the cot. 'She took the baby to hospital.' – hospital?' 'Cabeesh, 'ospitahl.'

'The father – papa? – caught the snake and took it to the hospital too'.

'Tony, what she say?'

I repeated and Tony translated. Romolo listened intently.

'Well, the parents waited while the doctors looked at the baby,' – Tony translated – 'and then the doctors came out and said, "The snake didn't bite the baby, the baby bit the snake!" I watched Romolo's face as Tony translated the end of the story. I was rewarded by the illumination of his face by that dazzling smile.

Tony was tired of translating, so he produced an Italian-English dictionary and we struggled on with that, the process becoming less efficient as we became more stoned. We found our communication difficulties uproariously funny. Eventually, the hilarity was worn out and so was I. I decided to go home. Romolo said he'd walk with me.

When we got to the entrance of Cairo, I stopped and turned to him. 'I come up,' he said.

'No, you go home.'

'I come up. For coffee.' I hesitated.

'I have joint.'

A night-cap would be nice. 'Okay, just for coffee and joint. Then home.'

He spread his hands as if to say: 'Of course, what else?'

Upstairs, I made the coffee in a metal coffee maker, which he examined approvingly. He seemed to find my method of fastening down the top of the coffee bag with a clothes peg a little perplexing but amusing. He did approve of the coffee, after taking a deep sniff from the bag.

The coffee banished my sleepiness. Campbell Parade was quiet. The beach was black but the sound of the waves ceaselessly creeping up the sand filled the silence between us.

At first I tried to think of something to say, but as Romolo seemed content sipping his coffee, sucking on the joint and listening to the ocean, I relaxed into the quiet.

As I passed him on my way back from the window, where I'd been enjoying inhaling the moist salty air and negative ions, he put his warm hand low on the softness of my belly and looked directly into my face with a very serious expression, an expression which said that desire is not something to be made light of. Recalling that moment afterwards, I could analyse the attraction: the serious, unabashed look and the place he chose to put his hand, that neglected erogenous zone, the true seat of womanliness, his unmistakable reverence for the feminine – all of this was unusual in my experience. But at the time, I was only aware of my desire rising to meet his, almost instantaneously. The strength of this response even survived his insistence that we both 'woosh' first. I didn't think too much about this; I was willing to remove any obstacle to the consummation of our desire.

I regretted his going home before morning, but I felt so contented and drowsy, I let it go and was soon asleep. All through the next morning, I remembered bits of the night before and smiled to myself. By afternoon, delicious reminiscence was shading into delicious anticipation. It felt like being in love. A week later I was sure that this was the real thing: Love.

'You're not in love,' scoffed Sally. 'You've just discovered sex, haven't you?' Sally was older and impressively worldly-wise, but I insisted that I was in love. When she saw him, she was impressed. He had a handsome face, dressed well and smelled wonderful. 'I can see why you think you're in love,' she said. 'He's a bit short for you though, isn't he?'

‘Not when we're both three feet off the floor,’ I retorted.

She laughed. ‘You *have* just discovered sex.’

Sally was the older sister of my old school friend, Philippa, and first flatmate. Phil said ‘How can you be in love with someone you can't talk to?’

‘We can talk.’

‘Not very well.’

‘Well enough. Love is beyond words.’

‘No it's not. Sex is beyond words. Love needs words. That's how you get to know the person.’

It was true that communication between Romolo and I was hampered by our preference to speak each other's language in order to learn it. One of Romolo's flatmates came in one day as we were sitting at the kitchen table, looking up our dictionaries.

‘What are you two doing?’ he asked.

We answered in unison without looking up. ‘Talking.’ I found the relationship exciting. I didn't see him as often as I would have liked, but often enough to keep my love, or whatever it was, alive.

During this period, I revived an adolescent habit of shoplifting. I'd come home with clothes for me and for him. I also got daily necessities like soap and shampoo. One day I brought back a silver sugar bowl which Romolo was very taken with and posted back to Italy.

I decided I wanted to have his baby. He was vehemently against the idea. 'Is no good. Baby need father. I go home in Italy two months. Is no good.' I didn't think much about his departure. He had talked to the other Italians about extending his visa; he might even stay. I thought about sticking a pin into the condom packet but decided against it. Instead, I put my faith in his ignorance of the potency of pre-ejaculation seminal fluid. So foolish, so well-informed.

Then my periods were late. I started to think almost realistically. How was I going to support this baby? I'd start stocking up straight away. I went to Grace Bros in Bondi Junction and stole some baby clothes. As I left the shop, an iron grip closed on my upper arm. It was not possible. It could not be happening. As the next hour passed, I was in an altered state of consciousness, suspended animation, observing disconnectedly as I was taken first to the Loss Prevention Office in the store, then to the police station. Sometime at the station I connected with the police officers, flirted with them, insisted on applying fresh lipstick for the mug shot, disagreed with them about my height and generally behaved in a way that they seemed to find somewhat unusual. At one point, I was alone with a police exhibit in a flowerpot so I quickly pinched off a few leaves.

When they let me go, I went home, dried the leaves in the oven and went around to Bill and John's to share the joint and the story. They didn't find it as amusing as I'd shaped it to be. As I stood outside their door taking my leave, Bill said 'I don't follow. I can't follow. You've gone somewhere I can't ... can't follow.' Bill prided himself on a lack of moralism. This was as close as he'd come to disapproval. But neither Bill, nor the experience of being caught, nor the late arrival of my periods, stopped me from shoplifting.

I got caught twice more. Once at David Jones Elizabeth Street Store. The value of the goods I was caught with was $997. The police thought I must have a calculator on me. If the value had been over $1,000, I would have been charged with a more serious offence, and the case heard in a higher court. They could not have been more misguided in their assumptions. Calculation was completely absent from my actions; they were entirely impulsive. Where those impulses came from, I never stopped to think. I thought I was having fun. Getting caught was less traumatic now that I knew the routine.

My friends struggled to understand my behaviour. After dinner one night at Elisabeth's, she asked, 'What is it you've been taking?'

'The first time was baby clothes.'

'Baby clothes!'

'Well, I thought I was pregnant at the time. False alarm, it turned out.'

'Ye-es, and the other times?'

'Clothes, make-up, jewellery, lingerie...'

She ruminated in silence for a few moments.

'They're all things to do with your femininity. Do you feel you have to steal those things because you're not entitled to them legitimately?'

I felt embarrassed and flustered at this line of thought, although I had spoken frankly with Elisabeth about every other topic under the sun.

'Oh, I don't know,' I said in a flip tone, 'Freud said it was all about sex, didn't he?'

'I think Freud said everything was all about sex,' said Elisabeth, before allowing the conversation to change course.

Philippa was interested in the details, but not the motivation. 'Why ever it is you're doing it, you've got to stop. You're going to get into big trouble. What if you go to prison?'

'I don't think I will.'

'How do you know? If you did it often enough, I'm sure they'd send you to gaol.'

Travelling in the back of a taxi one day with Bill, I saw something written in his large, loopy handwriting on a manila folder he was carrying. I read it aloud:

'Going too far is just another way of holding back.'

Bill smiled at me. 'It's true,' he said. I turned this sentence over in my mind for days, trying to grasp its meaning, but it was as if my brain lacked the sophistication of circuitry required.

The time for Romolo's departure was looming. He'd spoken a few times about staying and even my coming to Italy. 'You can be baby-sitter for my children.'

But none of it had happened and in a few days he would fly away from me.

The others all went to the airport with him. I said goodbye at Cairo. I was so distressed at his leaving that I didn't trust myself not to make an embarrassing scene at the airport. It is hard to believe that I could have so lost myself in what now seems a slight relationship. But then I had no basis for comparison. I remember being in the bank one day, filling out my forms and singing the Foreigner song:

I want to know what love is
I want you to show me,
I want to know what love is,
I know you can show me.

An older woman, that is, a woman in her thirties, was smiling at me. Because I didn't understand her smile, I stored it in my memory. Now it is my smile, as I remember that young woman singing in the bank, uninhibited and open to love. I thought what I felt for Romolo was love and maybe it was. Maybe it's a mistake to let the light of later more mature loves shine too harshly on that one. I learned from it that you can give your heart and survive, but also the high cost of that reckless generosity.

I cried all day the day he left. Some of the others called in on the way back to see if I was all right. We smoked some dope, but it didn't help. I went to bed early and cried myself to sleep. The next day I got back into life but would cry at odd moments.

Three days later, I was distracted by my first court appearance. I got dressed up in respectable clothes, stockings and high heels, all stolen, and waited in line for the duty solicitor. He took one look at me and sent me to the court social worker. She said: 'You don't present like the people we're used to here. You're well-dressed and well-spoken. Do you mind telling me why you took the items you stole?'

‘I just wanted them.’

‘I think there was probably more to it than that. I'm going to ask the magistrate to hold your case over until we can get a Pre-Sentence Report.’

‘Okay,’ I said, offhandedly.

But when the magistrate said that he didn't see the point of a Pre-Sentence Report and couldn't we just deal with it then and there, I was on the edge of my seat. When the social worker replied, her firmness was like two strong arms of support around me.

‘Your honour, I believe that there are special circumstances in this case which need to be brought before the court. I see a clear need for a Pre-Sentence Report.’

‘Very well,’ he grumbled, ‘will six weeks be sufficient?’

On the bus home, tears rolled down my cheeks silently, effortlessly. They were for Romolo. My legal troubles were already forgotten. A slip of paper in my wallet contained a phone number I had to ring. My mind was free to sink into contemplation of loneliness. I let the tears roll down till they cooled on my chin and dropped. A woman gave me a tissue as she got off the bus. ‘You poor girl,’ she said feelingly.

My friends were less sympathetic. They were impatient with my grief. Philippa remonstrated with me. ‘Can't you just see it as a holiday romance? I mean I know it was exciting and everything, but it was never going to last. You must have known that. Can't you just remember the fun you had and get on with it? You know, “Pick yourself up, dust yourself off and start all over again”.

It was to be a few months before I was ready to do that.

I distracted myself from my loneliness by resuming the renovation project that had been interrupted by my romantic and criminal exploits. The floors had been a disappointment. They were timber, of course; I had checked a corner before I pulled up the carpet. But they were grimy with accumulated dirt, covered by some black substance that could have been old lino glue. I didn't know what to do with them so I just got used to being unable to walk around in bare feet. Romolo had made disgusted 'tch' sounds whenever he contemplated it. He'd worn Scholls sandals around the flat so that he could negotiate his track from bedroom to bathroom and back easily. I always had a pair of thongs handy for the same purpose. Thinking back, I don't remember trying a scrubbing brush and I can't think why not. Surely if feet picked it up, then warm soapy water would have shifted it. I wasn't strong in practical skills. In fact, I don't recall at that stage owning a bucket. Eventually, I got sick of it and bought a tin of grey paving paint. I just slapped it down on the kitchen floor without any preparation beyond sweeping. It was nice to have one floor that felt smooth and clean under my feet. But to my surprise, the paint started to wear off before long.

I called the Probation and Parole Office. They made an appointment for me with my very own Probation and Parole Officer called Ken. He took down the basics of my life story and sent me up the road to the Community Health Centre to see a counsellor. 'Bob's our specialist in shoplifters,' he said cheerily. 'A report from him, attached to my report, could help your case.'

So I would be seeing a counsellor, the course of action I had resisted so strongly during what was generally considered to be my nervous breakdown, the condition which had led me back to my family home. Now, in the sobered frame of mind the loss of Romolo inspired, I had the sense to be concerned about the outcome of my case, and if Ken said seeing Bob would help, I was prepared to overcome my reservations. The fact that my capitulation was neither entirely voluntary nor entirely forced somehow made it more acceptable.

Bob made it easy. Even suicide was discussed in a light, conversational tone.

'And have you ever had suicidal thoughts?'

'Yes, when I was at Lane Cove I did.'

'Ever come close to acting on them?'

'No, I bought lottery tickets.'

'Lottery tickets?'

'Yes. I knew I'd never do it as long as there was a chance I could have won the lottery. As soon as I found out that my ticket hadn't won, I bought another one. It was a good system.'

'So you never really wanted to die.'

'Yeah, sometimes I did, but I was never sure it was the right thing to do. I was always afraid that I'd realise too late that it was a mistake, like half way down the cliff.'

'That's how you would have done it? Jumped off a cliff?'

'No, no, I'm too cowardly. No, I was never serious enough to actually plan it. I only thought about deciding to do it.'

'I had a client once who jumped off The Gap.'

My eyes widened. 'He died?'

'He didn't?'

'No. A huge freak swell came in just as he jumped and pulled him out. Then another wave deposited him on the rocks and he walked away with a few cuts and bruises.'

'Really? Did he try again?'

'Nup. He said: "That's it. I'm not meant to go," and he's never tried it again.'

'That's amazing.'

'So, the suicidal thoughts you had when you were back at your Mum and Dad's, was that the first time you'd had those thoughts?'

'Oh no. The first time was when I was ten.'

I was quite proud of this precocity. I thought it showed that even at that age I was a dissenter, rebelling against life, like Janis Joplin. Bob made a note of it but didn't seem particularly impressed. He asked about the shoplifting episodes and my shoplifting history.

'How did your Mum and Dad react when you were caught?'

'Oh, I didn't tell them.'

'Aaah. People usually don't.'

'Don't what?'

'Don't tell ... the person involved.'

During the third visit he asked in his usual casual tone, 'So why did you pinch all this stuff?'

'Because I wanted it.'

'Okay, so why did you start getting caught?'

I hadn't thought of it like that. I was less certain. 'Bad luck?'

'You don't think you were being just a bit reckless?'

I shifted uncomfortably. 'Yeah, I suppose I was.'

'Recklessness is a symptom of depression.'

'I wasn't depressed. I was having a good time.'

'Hmmm. Well I'll send a report up to Ken. When do you go back to court?' He looked at me searchingly.

'The 29th of July.'

'How do you feel about that?'

'I don't know.'

'You seem a bit down.'

'That's because I miss Romolo.'

'Oh yes, Romolo.'

He stood up. 'I'll send the report on. I don't need to see you again, but if you want to call in for a yarn, just give us a ring.'

I remained seated, reluctant to give up his kind and calm attention.

He sat down again and opened his appointment book.

'Do you want to arrange a time?'

I hesitated. If I saw him voluntarily, I would be admitting that I wasn't okay, that I needed help.

'It's up to you,' he said. 'I think it would be helpful to you to talk a few things through. But you don't have to decide now. Think it over and give me a ring.' He closed the diary and stood up again.

'I'll make a time now,' I said.

He sat back down and opened the appointment book, without betraying a hint of impatience. As I walked to the bus stop, I felt pleased with my decision.

All my legal papers found each other and the three charges were heard together at Bondi Junction Courthouse. The magistrate kept everyone waiting while he read through the reports from Ken and Bob. Then he. addressed me. 'Miss Gentle, all parents hope for great things from their children. But you have to decide what's important to you. If that's being the best secretary you can be, there's no need to let other people's expectations deter you. I hope you'll think about what I've said.'

'Boring old fart,' I thought, 'what would he know?'

'Now, as to the sentence, I am imposing a Community Service Order of 100 hours, which will be supervised by the Department of Probation and Parole.'

Well, it could have been worse. The Duty Solicitor agreed. 'Do it again, though, and I'll have a hard time keeping you out of gaol.' Ken also agreed that it was a good result. He arranged for me to read tapes for the blind. It seemed a good idea, especially as it would not involve me identifying myself in public as a wrongdoer. But the book I had to read was a Hare Krisna tract, full of the unpronounceable names of an Indian spiritual hierarchy and I found it very difficult. I suppose it was a fitting penance, to help a blind seeker after truth.

During my whirlwind romance and legal problems, I had let the petty details of life, like my finances, slide. Now, just when it seemed all the drama was over, my day to day life became a drama. My rent was in arrears; the gas, electricity and phone companies were threatening disconnection. I got angry letters in the post. My situation seemed precarious, alarming. I told Bob about it during one of our regular weekly appointments. He didn't seem too concerned. 'So what are you going to do about it?'

'I suppose I'll have to get a job,' I said gloomily.

'Can you get one just like that?'

'I always have before.'

I rang Templine. I preferred temporary work. Even if I stayed a year, each week of the 52 I could leave, in theory at least. The agency rang every Thursday morning to get my hours and ask if I wanted to go back the following week. Templine was a bit different. It catered to the Government departments and offered longer-term jobs.

'This one, they want to interview you,' the clerk said. 'It's for two months. Secretary to the Secretary of the Education Commission.' The following afternoon, I found myself waiting in surroundings that my recent history made seem somewhat plush. A nuggety woman with short grey hair strode towards me on hockey player's legs.

After we introduced ourselves, she came straight to the point. 'Now tell why I should give you this job.'

'I'm not saying you should,' I replied, somewhat taken aback.

She looked a bit put out, but not fazed. 'Let's start again. My secretary has gone to Italy for two months to find her roots. I suspect she'll find she's more Australian than she thinks, but nevertheless, she has gone and I need to replace her. There's not much typing. I delegate most of the correspondence to others. However, a lot of mail comes across my desk. It needs to be dealt with promptly: circulated, delegated, filed. Think you can manage that?' I didn't think the job would extend me unbearably, so I was hired.

The job was not too bad. It was at Circular Quay and I enjoyed going down to the harbour at lunchtime and eating my sandwich while watching the seagulls, smelling the briny air and hearing the sound of the ropes straining to hold the moored ferries. The fact that I was working full-time and doing all I could to resolve my financial problems meant that I didn't worry, and those lunchtimes were brief periods of tranquility.

At home, however, my chickens had come home to roost. My first paycheck had not arrived in time to forestall the gas company, and the gas had been cut off. Each time I raised the money to pay the bill, they added on another charge. With no hot water, and a job to be presentable for each weekday, I had to shower at the Biltmore each night. Although Mrs Crate's cheery salutations always lifted my spirits, it was a punishing routine. I'd found that going down there in office clothes didn't work. As it made no sense to change back into them I started to change into other clothes before I went.

So I'd get home, have some dinner, change into my showering clothes, sally forth to the Biltmore, come home and maybe have time for a brief chat with Bob-next-door before it was time for bed.

I asked Mum to help me with the gas bill. She said I needed to learn to balance a budget. She called around one day with a small electric jug. She'd found it at a white elephant stall. It still had $2 written on it in black texta.

'What am I supposed to do with this?'

'You said you had no hot water.'

'And I'm supposed to fill the bath with an electric jug?'

She seemed to find my reaction ungracious.

Going to the Biltmore every night, smelling that corridor smell, was becoming depressing. I was beginning to dread it in spite of Mrs Crate, who had become the soul of geniality since my rent had started coming in regularly. Finally, I rang the gas company and told them I'd just moved in and wanted the gas connected. I gave my name as Joy Fuller (Mrs). Within a few days, I was showering in my own flat. I wished I'd thought of it earlier.

Meanwhile, the Secretary and I were adjusting to each other. One day she called me into her office. 'The Chairman's secretary is having a flexi-day on Friday. As you may have noticed, she usually brings the Chairman's lunch in to him on a tray with a cup of tea. So on Friday, someone else will have to bring in the Chairman's lunch. I was wondering whether you might agree to do it?'

I had long since developed a policy of refusing to make tea. As a temp in the era immediately following the demise of the institution of tea-lady, it was very easy to be finessed into making tea on the first day and then find yourself cast as office drudge for the duration. So I'd developed a technique of smiling regretfully and saying 'I'm sorry, I don't make tea,' which unaccountably proved to be an unassailable position. But this was not the first day, and it was not the default tea-maker asking me, so I was caught off-guard. My face felt hot with indignation but my voice sounded icy as I heard it say, 'If I wanted to be a waitress, I wouldn't get up so early in the morning.'

The Secretary froze for an instant, and then, for the first and last time, I saw her flustered. She quickly rose to her feet and ushered me out saying, 'Well, for God's sake don't tell the Chairman that.' I heard no more about it, but as I went out to commune with the gulls on Friday, I saw the next most senior secretary bustle in to the Chairman's office with a tray.

I was living on a very tight budget, most of my wages going to pay the old bills. One night, Steven downstairs asked if I wanted to go to a cabaret show his boyfriend was performing in. When he said the admission was $4, I hesitated. 'Anyone can afford $4,' he said. But it took a major re-juggling of my budget to release that $4.

I'd known Steven before I'd moved into Cairo. He'd been visiting me when he'd first seen his flat. It was the grandest in the building. It was the largest and it had dark carved woodwork around the windows and shelves. He was tall and flamboyant and the flat suited him. He liked to spin romantic speculations as to how it came to be ornamented as it was. 'I'll bet it was a bookie's flat,' was one explanation.

Sometimes, as I trudged up the stairs, he'd invite me in for a drink. He was curious about my new life. 'It's so quiet up there,' he said. 'It's like sitting on a time bomb.' Once, when he was away, he sent me a postcard, a retro image of a scarlet woman, with the caption: 'She was tired of being good.' Well I wasn't. Not yet. Structure and stability, the virtuous whittling down of my debts - it felt like what I needed.

I had become a weekend renovator. I would wake up late on Saturday mornings and the light pouring into the flat would inspire me with visions of how great it would look when I'd fixed it up. The hated carpet was long gone, pity about the floorboards. Now I turned my attention to the walls. I set to work removing the wallpaper so I could paint the walls white.

The hall was the worst. The wallpaper there had a geometric pattern in lime green, yellow and orange. There must have been a time when prevailing notions of style allowed it to please someone's eye, but I found it hard to imagine. Every time I saw it in a good light it oppressed me. I would pick up the scraper, kept handy for the purpose, and scrape away at it. But again I was defeated by the age of serious glue. In the other rooms, there was a point at which scraping ceased and the paper peeled off in long strips. But here, every square inch of it was securely fixed.

The way I approached it varied. Sometimes I would make patterns through it with the scraper and then scratch out the little islands I'd made. Other times I'd concentrate on one little patch and systematically work away at it. After an hour or two, I'd be rewarded with maybe four square inches of exposed wall, painted yellow, with a few scratches and dents where the scraper had gone through to the plaster. It was a discouraging task and would be abandoned for weeks at a time in favour of other jobs that offered quicker gratification, like painting a window frame.

Philippa called over one day and looked around. 'Why don't you just cover it all in white paint?'

'I'm going to, but I have to get rid of the wallpaper first, and it's taking a really long time because it's stuck on with old-fashioned wallpaper glue.' Philippa was impatient with my explanation. 'Then don't scrape it off, just paint over it.'

'I suppose I should have done that to start with, but it's too late now. It's half scraped off and there are these bits with lines scraped through the paper.'

She was almost angry. 'It doesn't matter,' she said, with slow deliberate emphasis. 'Just paint over it. The main thing is to get it all one colour. You'll never notice the texture. It's looking at all these different surfaces that's driving you crazy.'

I ignored her advice. Philippa, being a painter, I reasoned, placed an exaggerated importance on visuals. It was a small step from a professional bias to a theory of defective decor as the root of all human suffering. But she was right about one thing. Although I wasn't always certain I was going crazy, something wasn't right with me.

I'd started to get back in the social swim. I was getting over Romolo. I reported a dream to Bob the counsellor, whose interest in dreams was disappointingly minimal. 'I dreamed I had my foot cut off.' He gazed out the window. 'You suffered a loss.'

'And then I built a little platform for the stump to rest on. I attached it to my leg and then I could get around perfectly well.'

Bob suppressed a yawn and examined his fingernails. 'So you've compensated for the loss and adapted yourself to it.'

'And then I dreamed I was in bed and I remembered how I used to rub my feet together and I thought "I'm going to miss being able to rub my feet together".'

'Well, I think we both know what *that* bit is about.'

I hadn't known until he pointed it out and to cover my confusion, I took out a cigarette. Now he was interested. He leaned forward and narrowed his eyes. 'You're smoking again.'

I had stopped smoking a few days after Romolo left. My reasoning was that if I could stop at a time like that, what could ever induce me to start again?

'Yeah, I was at a dinner party, and I'd been drinking quite a bit and when I got the craving for an after-dinner cigarette, I convinced myself I could limit it to one a day, after dinner. It's already gone from as many as I like after dinner to only after work. Soon I'll be having one with breakfast again.'

Bob dismissed my ruefulness. 'I think it's a good sign. There was something self-punishing about the way you gave up,' he said, pulling on a B & H. 'How was the dinner party?'

'It was fun. I had a great time.'

'So you're back in the land of the living.'

'Yeah, I suppose so.'

And yet it was at this time that I began to suffer from short bouts of what even I could recognise as depression. I'd get a heavy leaden feeling one afternoon, and the next morning I couldn't face work. I'd spend good daylight hours in bed, avoid going out and have trouble doing anything, the simplest thing. If it involved any co-ordination of tasks, it'd take me ages. Deciding anything took me ages. Should I ring work? What should I say? Would they believe food poisoning again? I'd still be mulling over those questions at 11 a.m., but now with a new set. Is it too late now? Is late really better than never? Do I need an excuse for why I didn't ring earlier? Would they believe I overslept after a night of food poisoning again?

Sometimes I'd pace around agitated, other times I'd crawl into bed with a book and block out the world. Sometimes I'd do one and then the other. The depression would turn my thoughts completely negative. Any contemplation of the past or the present would be coloured by the bleak feelings of the present. I could see no hope for myself.

When I saw Bob the counsellor in this state, he would often ask, 'Are you worried about yourself?' which was a coded way of asking if I had any inclination to end my life. One evening he said, 'Do you remember when I was writing my report for Ken, and you told me you'd first had suicidal thoughts when you were ten years old?'

'Yeah, I did.'

'Tell me a bit about that.'

'Well, we were living in this little flat in Mosman, waiting for Mum and Dad to finish saving the deposit for the house. The flat only had a small hot water tank so we had to have quick showers. Mum used to signal us to get out by turning a tap in the kitchen that made the shower go cold. One night I was in the shower – it was the middle of winter – and the water went cold when I'd just put shampoo in my hair. I called out to Mum to turn it off but she mustn't have heard me. By the time I gave up I was cold already, but then I had to rinse out the shampoo in cold water. When I got out …'

'You must have been furious.'

'... I was freezing. I was impatient to get into my clothes, so I didn't take time to dry myself properly and so the clothes stuck to me and got twisted around and I was hopping around the bathroom getting more and more worked up. When I came out of the bathroom I was hysterical. Mum couldn't work out what could have happened. I'd gone into the bathroom a normal ten-year-old and come out a basket case. She kept asking me what was wrong and finally I just yelled at her, "I wish I was dead!" So that's the first time I had suicidal thoughts.'

The depressive bouts usually only lasted two days, with one off work. By the third day, I'd feel all right, and sometimes quite good, like I'd been through some purification ritual. But that summer, I had a bad stretch. I couldn't sleep. For three weeks, all I could do was doze. Every night I'd climb into bed exhausted, thinking 'Tonight I must sleep', only to spend another eternity shifting around a hot bed. Towards dawn I'd doze, but with the light I'd start up, instantly wide awake, but utterly unrefreshed.

Philippa seemed to blame the flat. Most of my friends were at a loss as to what to do or say or suggest. Not that I sought them out. All I cared about was sleep. I was postponing my life until I'd had a good night's sleep. I wasn't working. After the last job finished, I didn't take another one. It was becoming too difficult to keep it all together.

Bob-next-door's flat mate Caroline wasn't at a loss at all. Her only problem was that she could never focus her bountiful energies and talents on one task long enough to complete it before a new inspiration diverted her. 'Come for a walk,' she'd coax. 'Don't wear your shoes. Walk on the grass. You've spent too long walking on concrete. Concrete is the barrier we put between ourselves and God.' When I resisted she'd say, 'It's no wonder you can't sleep, you're not doing anything.'

'But I'm so tired.'

'Your mind is tired but your body isn't. We'll tire out your body and then you'll sleep.'

Once she wore me down and I went for a walk with her. I felt raw and conspicuous, like a snail without a shell, and I longed for the sanctuary of Cairo and the protection of my shoes. The walk didn't seem to help me sleep any better either.

Only once did I find something to help me sleep. There was a joint that had been sitting on top of the fridge since this episode started. I hadn't smoked it because I didn't like to smoke when I was depressed. It usually made me feel worse. One night my eye fell on the joint and I decided to smoke it. Afterwards, I fell into a deep sleep for four or five hours. For half a day I felt rested and refreshed, but then the terrible hyper-alert fatigue set in again.

Bob the counsellor wanted me to see the Community Health Centre's psychiatrist. I knew why. He wanted me to take anti-depressants. I wasn't going to. I'd seen *One Flew Over the Cuckoo's Nest.* No little white pills for me. But the sleeplessness wore me down. I couldn't think straight. I saw the psychiatrist and got the pills.

The pills got me back to work. Templine found me a job as Theatres Secretary at Sydney Hospital. Although it felt good to be sleeping again, I didn't feel healed. I envied the patients. I fantasised about collapsing in the hospital grounds and waking up in a white world with white nurses looking after me. The pills gave me a persistent feeling of disconnection from my own reality, as if I were living in the attic of my life, sensing what I thought of as my real life going on underneath, but unable to see it or experience it. I disliked this sensation, and as soon as I'd had a few weeks of good sleep, I stopped taking them. Bob wasn't pleased. 'You'll take anything if it's self- prescribed,' he muttered.

While I was working in Theatres, a 19-year-old boy was brought in with both legs gone. He'd been to an office party on Friday night and had had a lot to drink. While waiting for his train at Martin Place Station, he'd sat on the edge of the platform swinging his legs. He continued to sit there as the train came in. He was on the Operations List many times. 'Repair and Debridement of Stumps,' I'd type. I saw him once, being pushed around the hospital in a wheelchair. He still had a stunned look on his face.

His story echoed around my mind persistently. I told Bob about it. He looked at me through eyes narrowed against the smoke he was exhaling. 'How does it make you feel?' he asked.

'I don't know,' I answered, with barely suppressed annoyance. Bob was always asking me how I felt about things and I could hardly ever tell him. 'I just think about it a lot. How he could have been so drunk he wouldn't know to get up, and it is now that one mistake has changed his life forever.'

After about three months of working in Theatres, I became tired of it and told Templine I wanted a change. They rang back and said Personnel wanted to talk to me about it. So I rang Personnel.

'I understand you don't want to continue working in Theatres,' the Personnel Officer said.

'That's right. I'm getting bored with it now.'

'Is it just Theatres you're bored with, or the Hospital in general?'

'Just this particular job.'

'Well, we need someone in Pharmacy. It's more clerical than secretarial. Would you be interested in that?'

I took a few seconds to weigh up the pros and cons. 'Yes, all right.'

'Now we'll need you to train the new Theatres Secretary. Could you stay there until we find someone to replace you – it shouldn't take long – and then train her before you start in Pharmacy?'

I agreed, but I was surprised they thought my replacement would need training. I hadn't had any. When I started, the previous secretary had left abruptly and no one had been sure exactly what she'd done. I just worked it out as I went along. So I was even more surprised to discover how complex the job really was and that it was a very busy two days I spent training the new secretary. The first day I had her follow me around watching what I did, and the second day I followed her around watching what she did. She picked it all up very quickly and was extremely grateful that I was there to train her for this complicated job.

This was duly related to Bob, who smiled. 'So they've got you training staff now.'

'Well, it was just showing someone how to do my own job. But I quite enjoyed it in a way. Seeing her master it all.'

'So what are your thoughts about work? What would you really like to do?'

'I don't know. Nothing I like doing earns money.'

'You like reading, you like writing. I can see you as a Lecturer in English Literature or something like that.'

'I couldn't.' I laughed. 'But now you mention it, I've been thinking of going to University doing Arts.'

Bob gave a nod that meant he thought it was a really good idea but he didn't want his approval to stop me.

'Checked the closing date, have you?' he asked. 'It's usually the end of August.'

'Yeah, I rang UCAC and they're sending me the form.'

Bob looked impressed.

'Well, it doesn't mean I have to do it. It's just a form.'

'That's right,' said Bob, putting out his cigarette and getting up. 'It's up to you.'

Allison Gentle

a door opens

a door opens
and a stray emotion
stalks into your heart
makes its presence known
- whoa!
before you know it,
the furniture has been moved around,
the curtains taken down,
and
you can feel
something
going on, but
what's happening?
how
did this feeling
sneak through
where did it come from?

I hear birds singing
the rustling trees whisper words of peace
and beauty.

this is no dream.
I sit in my chair
let the music embrace me
why shut
the door
my heart is open.

helena wong
15 june, 2003

A Girl In The Outback

Running away

I had been leaving home all my life. When I was fifteen months old my mother found me at the bus stop dressed in nothing - except her handbag and high heeled shoes – and brought me home.

'You are a very naughty girl. You are not to go away without telling me. I don't know where you are,' she scolded. Again and again.

Then one Sunday when I was 18 months old my father built a six-foot high gate with sharpened pickets at the top, and I went over that the next day. After that when she came to get me it was the wooden spoon on the back of my legs, her tears of powerlessness, and sometimes the police.

Until I was eleven or twelve years old I never knew my destination. Then suddenly I did. I was going to the Outback. I read Mrs Aeneas Gunn's books, *We of the Never-Never* and *The Little Black Princess* and it opened up for me the possibility of enormous spaces and freedom of land and sky in inland Australia. I decided that I was going to leave for the Outback – soon. And it became my obsessive passion.

'Mum, I really want to go to the outback.'
'Yes, dear, now finish your homework and go to bed.'
'Where should I go, Queensland or the Northern Territory?'
'I really don't mind, just finish your homework, it's late.'
'How soon can I go?'
'As soon as you have the money, that's enough now go to bed.'

I read greedily all the poetry and every author writing fiction and non-fiction about inland Australia. There was Ernestine Hill, Frank Dalby Davison, Henry Lawson, Banjo Paterson, Thomas Wood, Eleanor Dark and Ion Idriess. Ion wrote books with titles like *In Crocodile Land.* I breathed in and out with the characters and my blood flowed with their lives. That was the life I wanted! It was the Outback. What I yearned for most was to live on a huge cattle station – really huge – about one million acres or more. I read of stock camps, mustering, land with no fences, stores every six months, droughts and floods, the smell of the dust and mastery of horses. I didn't want to live on a sheep station and I wanted Aborigines living where I lived since in all the books I was reading they seemed wonderful and mysterious.

Then when I was 14 years old I wrote to Ion Idriess.

> *Dear Ion,*
>
> *I think your books are wonderful and I really love the outback and I want to go and live there ... soon.*
>
> *Yours sincerely,*
>
> *Rosemary Morrow*

I received a very helpful positive reply from him, which said:

> *Dear Rosemary,*
>
> *Well, then I think you should go.*
>
> *Kind regards,*
>
> *Ion*

Then I had an adolescent burst of Christianity. Two things happened. One was the school holidays and a lovely long hot summer that I spent walking through the bush from Castlecrag to Northbridge harbour baths and return. One day I stopped on a grey sheet of flat Sydney sandstone and with the warmth on my back and legs I sat down. The temperature was perfect and the smell of the eucalyptus was heady. I was calculating how long it was before I could leave home. Then I had a spiritual experience and thought that Jesus spoke to me.

'Jesus I will dedicate my life to You,' I said, and when I stood up, I swear that I was floating above the ground. I think it was then that I gave my love, admiration and commitment to the natural environment. I saw it for the first time as a miracle and that feel never left me. The bush was more reliable and rewarding than the people in my life at that time.

Shortly after that Billy Graham came to Sydney, and one evening I went with my sister, Sidney, and was persuaded by the stars, darkness, his voice and the music to come forward for Jesus and be saved. Part of me really was against this yet part of me was mesmerised and so I walked down the long aisle and felt a bit stupid promising that I would give my life to Jesus. However as it was a promise, and then I took all promises seriously, I wrote in the back of my mother's old leather Bible that I had given my life to Him.

'I, Rosemary, hereby give my life to Jesus'.

Years later I ripped the page out when Sidney taxed me with not keeping to it and anyway I didn't have those beliefs any more.

Shortly afterwards I read Daisy Bates' book, *The Passing of the Aborigine*, and came down with a short, severe dose of missionary zeal. I wanted to go out to the Nullarbor Desert and live with a tribe of Aborigines as Daisy Bates did. I didn't know why living with Aborigines was so very attractive or even what Daisy Bates did there. I had no idea what 'helping' was and why she would be there helping THEM.

I talked to my mother in the kitchen after dinner as we made school lunches.

'Who is Daisy Bates and what does she do?'
'She is a sort of missionary who lives in the desert with a group of Aborigines and helps them.'
'I'd like to go and work there.'
'Well you have to go with a church. You have to be a deaconess.'

We talked about the difference between a minister and a deaconess.
'Then I want to be a minister.'
'You can't be a minister. You'd have to be deaconess.'
'Why can't I be a minister? I don't want to be a deaconess that sounds soppy and not as good as a minister'.
'Girls can't be ministers. So you'll have to be a deaconess.'

That evening I heard my mother and father laughing as she told him.

'Rowie wants to be a deaconess and live like Daisy Bates in the desert.'
'She wants to be a missionary?'
'Rowie wants to convert the Aborigines.'
'Is she going to serve Jesus as her Lord, then what about Peter who she says she's in love with?'

I muttered over my history assignment at the dining room table.

'I hate you all. I don't want to be a deaconess and I'm going to live on an outback cattle station for the rest of my life and never come home.'

The family ridicule burnt away that hope and my Christianity with anger and humiliation. My ardour wilted. Anyway Jesus let me down in lots of ways.

Time passed slowly at home as I waited for an opportunity to leave. For a short time my brother, Terry, was a jackaroo on a sheep station near Bourke in western NSW. He'd left home at 15 years old to train as a wool classer, and now he was on the sheep station. I considered briefly making my way out there and finding a life, but it was sheep and, with 150,000 acres, far too small, and I knew cattle were grander. However when he came home for a holiday and brought his stock whip, gaiters and saddle. I practised cracking his stock whip and polished his saddlebags and, breathing in the smell of dust, leather and polish, I thought: 'I am nearly there'.

My family was too pre-occupied with other dramas to give me much attention and so my determination was invisible to them. When I asked: 'How much does it cost to go to the Outback?' or 'How can I get to the Outback?' no one bothered to answer.

At school I was disruptive and inattentive. I was hard on the teachers because I could give excellent impersonations of them as well as of Elvis Presley and other stars. I could organise the class to have bottles of water circulating around the room under desks, and, for all pencil cases to fall on the floor at the one time. I was demoted as class captain when a new class teacher arrived and found 38 girls all trying to get around the classroom without putting a foot on the floor and in silence. They were standing on desks, hanging from picture rails, on the window sills and the teacher's desk.

At my best I sat at the back of the classroom and read books. After I was found with a copy of *The Sheik*, which I remember as mildly pornographic, I was brought down to the front of the class.

'Rosemary Morrow, where did you get such a book? No don't answer. Go immediately to Miss Ralston's office and tell her why I sent you.'

The book was confiscated, my parents asked to come to the school for another interview about my behaviour and I was told: 'Any more of this sort of thing from you and you will be expelled'.

My parents were handed the book and I later found it half-read on top of my parent's wardrobe.

No one ever asked: 'Why does she behave like that?'

I felt different from the other girls mainly because of my home life. I lied to my friends and told them how happy my parents were. I was secretly ashamed of them and most particularly my father. He was mean and bullied my mother. I felt I had to protect her. Dad and I were in constant conflict. His job was responsible and he wasn't coping very well. The atmosphere at his office was upper middle class and staffed by English men. Dad was a Redfern boy made good. I believe he felt inferior.

He was drinking a lot, becoming increasingly vulgar, burping offensively and slurping soup and soft foods, and wanting to hug me too much and hang around my bedroom and come into the bathroom. I fought back.

'Don't come into my room Dad, when I'm getting dressed.'
'Dad, knock when you want to come in to the bathroom.'
'Why can't you eat properly?'

'Don't you speak to me like that young Lady,' he would shout.
'I will if I want to.' And I would storm off.

I started to hate him and didn't want him anywhere near me. And I didn't like my newly emerging body and I decided to hide my femininity. Jeans and cropped hair didn't help me at all.

Mother, ever the ostrich, pretended none of this was happening.

'Mum, tell Dad to stay out of my bedroom.'
'Don't speak about your father like that dear,' she replied.

I shut the doors to my bedroom and bathroom and fixed them with chairs so I could hear if he was trying to open them and pretend he didn't know I was there. I avoided any physical contact with him because he clutched me too closely. I was deeply ashamed of my father. He always wanted to massage my chest with Vicks when I didn't have any illnesses.

'No, I don't need you to do that,' I would shout frantically. My mother said nothing.

I didn't invite friends home because of this shame and because I would have to protect them from my father.

So I stayed away from home as much as I could. The very early mornings I spent at North Sydney swimming pool, and afternoons on the tennis court. I always had friends and I spent a lot of time with them, but there wasn't one I could tell of my father's harassment or my Outback obsession because I felt it was silly.

Finally, I wandered blindly through my Intermediate Certificate and achieved quite well and then I was FREE for the holidays.

That Christmas I took a job with the Macquarie Travel Agents as a clerk and soon found that I had no aptitude at all for the work. It was years before I discovered and accepted that small fine detail was my weakness. Although I didn't like being in an office, that was when I discovered the City. I was smoking by then to show everyone (everyone older than me?) that I was grown-up. I enjoyed visiting the 'in' cafes that were just getting off the ground in Sydney at that time. I liked best the 'Poet and Peasant' and it was underground. It felt so mature to swing downstairs to a restaurant that had a cappuccino coffee machine, no windows and faintly arty table-cloths. I spent some wicked time up at King's Cross in a smoky dark upstairs cave sitting on cushions on the floor listening to folk singers. Finally the police came and said we must sit on chairs.

By the time school started again in 1958 I had managed to save from my wages the price of a plane fare to Darwin. I bought my ticket. I was finally going Outback. I didn't tell anyone at home because I knew there would be a big fuss about being 'so young' and hints about the terrifying dangers out there in the world for a young girl on her own. Home already had dangers. I told Sidney, who was a ground hostess with QANTAS in Darwin, that I was coming up there.

In early February three months before my 16th birthday I made my way to the airport and caught a plane to Darwin on TAA. My ticket was BH76511 and had cost £45 and two shillings.

The plane was small and plump and had big propellers and was probably a DC3. It was exceedingly slow and it took ten hours to get to Mt Isa where we refuelled. The terminal was a corrugated tin shed on a flat red plain and the temperature was close to 130°F. We waited and we waited. We didn't know why we were waiting. Someone brought us water. The delay was about fuel coming in 44 gallon drums from the township. It was boring. After five hours wait we finally took off and arrived in cloudy, sweaty, humid Darwin at 9.00 that night.

My first heady arrival in the tropics: the warm damp noisy air, insects, and smells and airports mingled as they would for the rest of my life. Sidney met me, thrilled I that I had come. She took me out to the staff compound at Berrima. I phoned my parents.

'Hello Mum.'
'Where are you Rosemary? We have been so worried.'
'I'm in Darwin.'
'Where?'
'Darwin, and Mum, I'm not coming back. I'm going to get a job on a cattle station.'
'Don't be silly, of course you're coming home, let me talk to Sidney.'
'She isn't here and I'm not coming home. I'm going to a cattle station.'

Mum burst into tears and said we would talk about it later.

In fact, despite a half-hearted threat to call the police, which would have been embarrassing for them if the neighbours had found out, I believe she realised that family life was going to be much quieter and easier at home less one difficult daughter and without the fights that erupted daily between me and my father. The unacknowledged stress on her and the household would be eased. Perhaps she thought that I was better off too. I had a lot to think away.

I was a self-absorbed teenager and barely gave my mother another thought for the next few weeks. She never called in the police and never ordered me home again. Mother told me years later that she had had a 'sort-of' breakdown after I left.

Darwin, pre-cyclone Tracey, had a frontier town feel to it. It had wide, slow streets and was multicultural before the word was known. Stockmen, missionaries, Aborigines, Government staff in shorts and white short-sleeved shirts, white women in muumuus, miners, sailors and refugees from the south, all drifted about its hot streets. The overhead sun bleached the colour from the buildings and any white colours burnt out your eyes. There were large trees, wide verandahs and mosquito-netted rooms and canvas blinds. At that time Darwin was famous for having the greatest consumption of beer per head in Australia.

I didn't know how to get to the Outback from here but I knew I was close. I thought I wanted to go as far from towns as possible in the Northern Territory. And while I was searching for my chance I found a job with the Eagle Star Insurance Company. My job was to type insurance contracts and these had to be word and letter perfect. Under such pressure for perfection I always made errors usually just near the end of the contract which then had to be typed again. The boss told me: 'Miss Morrow, each contract costs 1/6d and you must stop making mistakes.'

Now I started making more and I began taking the botched contracts home in my handbag. I had to bring a bigger handbag. In the meantime I decided that I loathed insurance, being indoors and 9-5 work.

I walked in to my boss's office to resign, but he beat me to it.

'Miss Morrow, you are making too many typing errors in the contracts and you are too slow because you have to type each one twice or more. We must let you go.' I think he had noticed the huge decrease in the pile of contracts.

'I was just coming in to resign Mr Williams, because I don't like this type of work.'

However it was the first of two times in my life that I was sacked. It felt so good.

Next Sidney got me a job with QANTAS. On the staff residential base at Berrima there was a tin shed full of uniforms. QANTAS, like hospitals and armies, has uniforms to grade people because you simply can't tell from looking at them if they are important or not. Men wore shorts in blue and grey and black. Some wore overalls. Shirts were pale blue, grey, white (for pilots – who generally didn't get their uniforms from me). Women were cleaners, ground hostesses and cooks but no girls were yet engineers or trade apprentices. In those days security had barely been heard of and so there were no uniforms for this job or I may have got myself into trouble.

In the corrugated tin shed called the Uniform Department, I had shelves and shelves and shelves of all colours and types of clothes. It was an unusual boutique. Uniforms were issued after someone signed a chit saying that Bill or May could have a new uniform and I was responsible for issuing it. I enjoyed it. I was alone because it was not very difficult. I tried on almost everything and would wear a different uniform every day and, I thought, with panache. I enjoyed meeting the different staff on the base and also gave some uniforms away. Young men used to come and flirt with me and it was very congenial.

However I was still committed to living on a big cattle station. So I haunted the stock and station agents. These were small nondescript offices which appeared to do nothing except shuffle papers. However they were agencies for the stations' owners. Even at that time many stations were owned by overseas companies, whose motivation was profit and whose interest in the land or the people was slight. The stock and station agents saw to the finances and financial management on the stations, delivery of stores, and the appointment of managers, jackaroos, bore mechanics and so on. They liaised with the Sydney office and the stations. They sent the station profits back to London, and later to owners in Tokyo and New York.

Black Star Shipping Line, aka Lord Vestey who lived in London, owned many stations in the Northern Territory and the Kimberleys. Among them were Wave Hill, Nicholson, Gordon Downs and Sturt Creek. Of these, Gordon Downs and Nicholson were the showpieces. I would visit the office receptionist every time I was in Darwin.

Finally, it happened. I was walking past the window of the Agents for Vesteys and gave a wave at the typist. She came out and said: 'There is a job for a governess for two children on Gordon Downs Station 110 miles south of Hall's Creek. Below it is Sturt Creek Station and beyond it is the Tanami Desert. Do you want the job?'

Want the job? I nearly choked on my YES and although there were papers to sign and probably a contract all that is now a blur.

Getting there

The blur continued for about ten days and then I took all my possessions in a small bag and, cigarettes in my back pocket, went to Darwin airport to catch the Connellan's Airways plane to Gordon Downs Station. My dream was taking shape. The plane was tiny and had two engines. There were four of us and the pilot. We flew low over the land and it was bumpy. I felt very nauseous but I daren't say so in case they thought that I was feeble. It was the wet season and the country was flooded. Sheets and sheets of shallow golden apricot floodplains. The airstrip at Gordon Downs was a lake and so, unable to land, we diverted to put down on Nicholson Station. The pilot jumped out on the wing and then put a ladder to the door. I crawled down it. The air was humid and hot. It was good to be on land.

I was met by Arthur Renfry, the bore mechanic, and Jean Langdon, the Gordon Downs bookkeeper. We bounced in an old jeep over the muddy field with its tussocky grass while a stockman on a horse kept watch for cattle or kangaroos which might run onto the airstrip. I had never seen anything quite so beautiful in all my 15 years as this low roofed, one-storey homestead with its fly wired verandahs squatting on its green lawns, and around it a cluster of outbuildings whose uses I would later learn to recognise on all stations.

We had tea with the Nicholson manager's wife on the south verandah with pot plants in neatly painted red and green 44 gallon drums and scones fresh from the wood fired stove. The cement floor painted green shone with wax. We were served by Aboriginal women with bare feet and white uniforms.

I was besotted with absolutely everything. It was all perfect.

'Thank you,' I said, 'Yes, that's super,' and 'Yes I love the scones. Thank you.'

Then, looking at Arthur, Jean said, 'We must go now Rosemary. We need to travel as much road as we can in daylight because Sturt Creek has flooded five miles wide. Many of the jump-ups are running a banker. We'll come and visit Nicholson again one day.'

We left after exchanging mail bags and taking some fresh fruit from the pilot. He wheeled overhead as we set out over the wet slippery roads. It was 80 miles to my new home, Gordon Downs, and Nicholson was our closest neighbour.

I understood nothing and loved it all. Sturt Creek had flooded across a vast plain and looked like a flat pale creambrown lake. We travelled very slowly trying to stay on the camber of the road, which was covered in creamy orange mud, potholes and corrugations. I sat in the back in a mystical trance and tried to absorb everything through my senses – the red, wet mud and its smell, the exhaust of the car, the colours of the afternoon, the thick chunky black clouds and the flocks of birds, the warm humid air. The 'spat' as the wheels threw lumps of mud from the tyres to the mud flaps. At times we would stop at a 'jump-up', a gully where the water ran fast and to an unknown depth, and Jean would get out and walk across in the golden opaque water calling out about the hardness of the road and the speed and depth of the water. Then Arthur would rev the engine really hard to keep the water out of the exhaust pipe, and we would slowly and steadily get to the slushy bank on the other side. Sometimes we floated off the road – just a little, and I was oblivious to the real danger of being washed away.

I can't remember the hours passing, but until the streaky orange, fluorescent sun quickly dropped away I stuck my nose to the window and watched birds wheel, kangaroos leap away, and emus streak off on their long legs. Sometimes groups of cattle sat stubbornly on the road – it was drier than the paddocks – and refused to move until we were nearly on them with the bullbar. Then they raced off splashing, mooing, kicking and protesting. The 80 miles took till 10.00 pm and we slithered and slid at 10 mph and finally I dozed during the dark hours.

As we came to Gordon Downs homestead we saw the lights, heard the generator and the dogs were barking. We went slowly through the gates opened by Jean, got stiffly out of the jeep and then after meeting many new people I was shown to a two roomed corrugated iron building with a cement floor and two rooms opening onto a verandah. Its corrugated iron windows were held open with pieces of wood. These were the classroom quarters where I would live and work.

'Breakfast at 6.00 am,' the boss, Stan Jones, said as he shook my hand.

'School starts at 6.30 but tomorrow you can meet the children and talk to Mary, my wife, about your hours. The first waking bell is at 5.30 am and the second bell is at 6.00 am. You will eat with us in the homestead dining room. Welcome to Gordon Downs.'

I fell asleep immediately under my mosquito net in my fold-up iron bed, with its horsehair mattress, stiff, clean, cotton, white sheets and coarse grey blanket with a red stripe down the middle.

I awoke to the clanging of a gong. I sat up, looked out my window and saw what was the kitchen – a big corrugated iron shed. Scented smoke drifted from the chimneys and into my window. I inhaled deeply. Outside the kitchen an Aboriginal man was chopping wood and a fat man who looked partly Aboriginal and partly Chinese was banging with a long heavy old chisel on a bigger piece of iron hanging from the roof. It was 5.30 am and as I watched, several sleepy looking Aboriginal women strolled very slowly up to the kitchen door in response to the gong.

Some gong times were for the workers, some for stockmen and some for those who ate in the homestead dining room. We lived and worked to the gong.

Behind the kitchen with its half open fly-wired walls and only about ten metres from it, I could see a large square two storey house. The house was painted with white oil paint. The top part was all shutters and the bottom all open but fly wired in. I guessed that's where I'd go for breakfast.

My eye moved over the landscape. The sun was casting long, already warm shadows and there were lolly-pink clouds tinged with black. The homestead stood on and was surrounded by a beautifully manicured lawn. Early sprinklers were throwing spray over the lawn, which was bordered by a white painted log fence about waist height with special gates to allow people to enter and leave but not horses and cattle.

There was a gravel tennis court, which had been recently swept, watered and rolled. And the other side of this, a smaller cottage painted the homestead colours of pure white and edged with pillar-box red and bright glossy green. There were old large shady trees around the homestead, but the smaller cottage had no trees and the grass was brown.

I washed in cold water, agonised a bit about what to wear, what would make me look older, and decided on fresh Bermuda shorts and light shirt, then walked over to the big kitchen on the way to the homestead dining room. The kitchen had two enormous wood cooking stoves and there were basins of risen bread dough covered with tea towels made from flour bags. A yeasty smell filled the air. Henry Ah Chin, the cook, introduced himself.

'I'm Henry. I heard you was coming,' he said. 'It'll be nice to have a girl on Gordon Downs. Come 'n talk whenever you wanta.'

'That's a lot of bread you're making Henry.'

'Yairs, we make our own bread here, we cook eighteen loaves of bread every two days all year round. We feed 140 people a day. Some is for the blacks and the rest for the homestead and stockmen's dining rooms.'

I didn't have any sensible comment to make but that was a lot of people. Henry was fat and wore baggy shorts below his belly to his knees, a white singlet and thongs as his all year round uniform. He mopped his sweaty forehead constantly with an old flour bag. Stations vied with each other to get Henry as their cook. They liked him, and the stockmen, Aborigines and homestead staff didn't grumble about the food when Henry was in charge. I liked Henry too. He was funny and told funny stories.

Already it was uncomfortably hot in the kitchen. I was a bit anxious about being late.

'Where will I eat? Where will I find Stan and the children?' I asked.

'You cross the lawn on the gravel path, then go straight through that door, go through the first room and into the second room. You eat in the manager's dining room. That's the dining room for the toffs,' he said.

Not knowing who the toffs were I made my way along a path to the big house opposite.

The first room was a huge scullery where the manager's dining room crockery and cutlery was stored and washed up. Here three clean white dresses hung on pegs. A large rope hung from the ceiling beside a post. I didn't know what it was for.

I went through the scullery into a rectangular room furnished only with a dresser at one end with dishes on it and a long wooden table in the middle that seated about 30 people. It had a white tablecloth made from cotton sheets and the table was laid for ten people and a highchair. Three of its walls were metal fly wire and already the blowflies were buzzing around thickly outside. This was the regular mealtime chorus. I waited a moment, then some other people came in, and finally the family.

No one sat at the table until the family arrived. Then the others took their places. I didn't know where to sit so I stood back a bit. Stan strode to the carving chair at the top of the table and sat down.

'G'day Rosemary, did you sleep well? Good. Then please sit down over there and I'll introduce you.'

'Good morning everyone, this is Rosemary. She has come, as you already know, to teach Jennifer and Randall – who both want to learn, don't you children?'

‘Yes, Mummy has already been teaching us and I can write and count to 100,’ Jenny said.

Randall looked less convinced that this was what he wanted to do.

Stan always sat at the head of the table. Mary sat on his right and Jean sat on his left. Next to Mary the baby, Terri, was in the highchair. Then I sat next to Jean. Then three young children introduced as Lawrence 4, Randall 6, and Jennifer 8, sat beside me. The bore mechanic, Arthur I’d met yesterday. A young jackaroo, and a visiting German anthropologist from Bonn called Hans, all sat in correct order. When we had Company visitors from Darwin or Sydney, I was moved to nearer the bottom of the table and the visitors sat, according to the recognised hierarchy, closer to the top of the table.

I watched and waited. An Aboriginal woman appeared in one of the white dresses I had seen in the scullery, bare feet, damp sleek hair and carrying a huge silver platter covered with dry leathery steaks. She put this down in front of Stan. A second woman, dressed the same, appeared with a plate of congealed fried onions and placed these in front of Mary. Stan took the first of a pile of plates in front of him, speared a steak and placed it on the plate, then passed it to Mary, who added onions. Plates were handed out according to the social seating hierarchy. The baby, Terri Lorraine, was handed a slab of steak to chew on to exercise her newly emerging teeth. I’d never seen a baby chewing on a lump of steak before. The steak was leathery. It had been killed the afternoon before.

The first Aboriginal woman brought in and handed around from the right of each person a large oval plate piled with toast. The toast was cool and tasted strange. It turned out that the flour was old and full of weevils. I learned to dig out the small black specks with my knife and place them on my bread and butter plate. When guests came Stan made the same old joke about 'weevils adding protein'. Some deep yellow translucent butter, which looked and was in fact rancid, sat in a cut glass bowl. Dabs of apricot, marmalade and fig jams also sat jellylike in cut glass bowls. Then the women brought us tea, which was always fresh, very hot and strong and often flavoured with heaps of white sugar.

I went to pour myself some water.

'The gins will do it,' said Stan.

As one of the women bent to fill my glass I realised she had a special musty smell. I liked it and it made me feel I wanted to get close to her. However among the whites there was a ritualised conversation about how terrible the blacks smelt. I never said that I liked it because they smelt real.

I learned, from watching the Aboriginal women, that food is served to a visitor's right and dirty plates are taken from the left. I also learned not to touch the glass when pouring water from a jug. I learned, although not then required to practice them, how to do all these things silently. None of this etiquette was relevant to the lives of the women who laboured in the house but lived down beside the dry creek bed.

There was no choice of menu at breakfast, or in fact any meal.

At breakfast Stan talked with Arthur, Jean, and the jackaroo.
'Jean, there's David coming up from Sydney to inspect the books in about three weeks. Will they be ready by then?'
'Arthur, can you go out to one tree plain and see if the cattle there have water?'

'We've been having a bit of a wind drought recently and so the windmills haven't been pumping up water for the cattle. We need to check them frequently,' he explained to me.

I nodded wisely. I had never heard of a wind drought before. It was a completely new idea.

Mary fed the baby and the children were well behaved in front of their father.

'Lawrence, you can come with me out to the red plain hill camp today and give Rosemary some peace and time to get to know Jenny and Randall.'

Lawrence was torn between the pleasure of riding horses with his father and the interest of a day with me and the other children.

Then Stan left to give orders in the men's dining room, which was another corrugated room with a low ceiling attached to the kitchen. They ate the same food as we did but on a bare board table. The head stockman was in charge there. And there was more laughter there as well.

We drank our second cup of tea then left the table. Every day breakfast would be the same as that first day.

At 6.30 am I was asked to come to the downstairs sitting room to learn about my duties. Stan and Mary were both there, but I quickly recognised that it was Stan who had the authority.

'You will teach Randall and Jennifer, and sometimes Lawrence will join you,' he said.

'My wife has been teaching them but with managing the gins, the stores and the meals she is now too busy.' Mary was bright, acquiescent and smiley and I felt we could be easy friends.

'As you know you will be paid £10 a month and a fare back to Darwin for Christmas. You will eat with us. A gin will do your washing and ironing, clean the classroom and your quarters. For today, I suggest you unpack, look around so you are familiar with the station, check the work the children have been doing, and spend some time with them.

'Their school hours are from 6.30am to 11.30am and the afternoons are free. You have no other duties and we hope you will be happy here. By the way this is a dry station, which means no alcohol is to be brought on to the station, nor drunk here.'

'Gosh, someone to wash and iron my clothes, and clean my room!' I thought of how many years my mother had hounded me to do these things. I felt quite uncomfortable about it, especially as I'd have the afternoons free.

Mary left to go to the kitchen and Stan to the yards and I wandered out to explore. I wanted to break into a happy skip but was afraid someone watching me would think I was a child.

The green square created by the fertilised, mown lawn and white fence was immaculate. As the sun rose quickly overhead Aboriginal men appeared with hoses and hand watered the gardens. In the distance the bore pump engine purred away. Older Aboriginal men dug over garden beds. Another man chopped wood, and another was painting the white fence. Painting the house and fence was like painting the harbour bridge – it was never finished. Pot plants such as philodendrons and fishbone fern in red and green 44 gallon oil drums looked cool. Aboriginal women set up tables and chairs under the big trees and the whole effect was leisurely, orderly and peaceful. It was very quiet.

Trying to look as if I belonged, I wandered over to explore the buildings beyond the fence. First I visited Jean in her office. Through the door at the back of her office, she showed me into the huge, galvanised corrugated iron shed, again with push-out corrugated iron windows and furnished with shelves and shelves and shelves of goods. The place was dark and hot and rich in smells of leather, new fabrics, tea and tobacco and others I couldn't recognise. I wandered along the shelves looking at the bolts of fabrics (bought to sell to the Aborigines to make clothes) the stockmen's trousers, belts and shirts, the cattlemen's hats, bags and bags of flour, boxes of tea, cigarettes and raw chewing tobacco. There were crates of jam and butter. White flour in bags was piled nearly to the ceiling. There was all the food and materials we would need for six months until the next stores were shipped up from Perth and then trucked in from Wyndham.

I knew I would want to come back here many times but Jean was busy.

'Thanks Jean, what a smashing place! Can I come back again sometime?'

I sauntered on, taking care to appear nonchalant.

I found the forge and watched the men start the fire and pump the bellows - because it was the day to make horse-shoes fit each individual horse's feet. A mob of about twenty horses were already mustered in the horse yard for measuring and shoeing.

Then, more nonchalantly with a cigarette in my hand, I moved to my real destination, the cattle stockyards. There were cattle in the yard being separated for the day's castrating and branding. I met the white ringers and some of the Aboriginal stockmen standing on the ground in the dust, squatting or leaning on the fence rails. I loved the smell of the dust. Perhaps, finally, that was all I had come here for ... the smell of cattle and horses in yards, and wide open spaces.

The stockmen were all skinny and wore their belts low. Their boots were high-heeled for riding fast and turning hard in the stirrups. Hats were pulled low over their eyes. The head stockman had bandy legs, high-heeled boots with spiked spurs, moleskins from R M Williams, and a plaited kangaroo skin belt holding up his strides because he didn't have a belly to do it. He strolled over.

'G'day, are you the new teacher?'

'Yes, hello, I'm Rosemary, the governess. I'm going to teach Jenny and Randall,' I replied confidently. 'I've come from Darwin and before that Sydney.'

'Big place that Sydney I've heard,' he said. 'What was you doing there?'

'I worked for a travel agent in Sydney, and then an insurance company in Darwin.' I hoped he wouldn't ask how long because each job had been about seven or eight weeks and I got sacked from both.

'How many cattle and horses are there on Gordon Downs?' I asked to move on from that uncomfortable topic.

'Well, I reckon we have 500 horses, and about 10,000 heada cattle.'

I was thrilled. It was the same as all those books I had read, and now coming true for me.

'Canya ride?' he said.

'No, not really.'

'My word that's too bad, I reckon we'll have to fix that up,' he said. 'I'll look round for a nice little mare for ya.'

I strolled away from the stockyards trying to walk as if I had rider's bandy legs. I was euphoric. I knew I would be happy there. Even heaven couldn't match this life.

The machine shop was my next stop on my way back. It was a big mechanics garage with three walls covered with tools. There were more than 100 forty-four gallon drums of petrol inside a fence. Piles of tyres lay around. An old truck called the 'weapon carrier' was over the pit hoisted up by a giant winch. The mechanic and some Aboriginal men were working, and the mechanic explained:

'All the petrol and diesel vehicles such as tractors, landrovers and cars are mended here. We also have to keep the generator in good nick or we won't have electricity or power for the radio. We do the repairs on the bore pumps and also the radio. Drop in any time. It's good to have more girls on the station.'

I hoped I looked older than a 'girl'.

On the way back to the homestead I peered in at the meat house. This was a wooden building with walls only half way to the roof, the rest being metal fly wire. A thick and deep eaved roof kept the sun off the walls. It stood alone to keep it cooler and there were big peppercorn trees around it. A bullock was killed every seven to ten days. A huge tripod was erected, and the animal once shot was pulled up on its back legs, its throat was cut and it was bled. Then it was immediately cut open and the entrails given to the lubras, then the skin was taken off and left on the fence to dry. These skins were tanned and placed on the floors of living rooms and bedrooms.

Then the carcass was butchered into different cuts. Some were placed in deep saline solution and this would make corned beef. Others simply hung in the meat house. We ate fresh steak the first few days and then had curries, roasts, stews, cold meat and older steak. An old joke was:

'Never eat your own killers[1], because someone else is eating yours!'

However I believe that Stan killed only his earmark and brand.

I thought as I left: 'This is a really beaut place with so many interesting things happening here where I can see them and I want to try them all later on.'

I missed seeing the saddle shop, the men's quarters and the visitor's quarters – they were for tomorrow. I returned to the schoolhouse quite delighted. Gordon Downs was a real little village with trades and skills I hadn't seen at home.

In my bedroom I unpacked the few items I had brought. I lit a cigarette and went into the room next to my bedroom – this was the classroom. It had one bench and three small chairs, and a blackboard and chalk and a table for me. There was also a table at the back with children's books on it.

---

[1] The animal killed for the station staff.

I was utterly ignorant. I didn't have the slightest idea about how to teach children; what was involved in teaching children, and what standards would have to be met? Nor even the idea that the children's education was important. And I wasn't even worried.

Then I heard the clanging of the huge chisel on the piece of railway line, the gong. I looked out my door. The breakfast group were taking their seats, deck chairs and plantation chairs under a huge shady tree and a table was laid with a clean cloth. The Aboriginal women were bringing out big tea pots. There were fresh scones and johnny cakes. I joined them. This was smoko, morning tea, at 9.30 am.

'Well, now you have met everyone then,' said Mary, 'and is there anything you need such as toothpaste, soap?'

'No thanks,' I replied adding with sincerity. 'It's perfect.'

I was unaware that another 130 people lived down the creek barely 100 metres away and that most of the adults and some of the children worked for the station.

Mary poured the tea. They talked.

'How much rain did they get at Sturt Creek station last night?'

'How fast do you reckon the Creek is flowing?'

'Have you seen any cattle affected by tick?'

I listened, recognising the authentic talk from all my reading about the Outback, and I felt that I was becoming one of them.

Quite a lot of the time the Aboriginal workers were the topic of the talk. Again I listened.

'They brought in the wrong horses to the yard this morning.'

'Big Nellie is going to have another baby.'

'You'd think they could wash more often.'

I listened some more.

This is how Helen Frizell, from the Women's Day in her article *Oasis in the Lonely Heart*, described smoko when she visited Gordon Downs in August that year.

> *At first sight, the group of people sipping morning coffee could have been relaxing in a city garden. Deck chairs stood on green lawns; tall trees cast shade; plants grew in hanging pots and vine-covered trellises made cool arches.*
>
> *But fair-haired hostess, Mary Jones, finishing her second cup of coffee was a long way from any city. For the group was having 8.30 a.m. smoko at Gordon Downs, a million acre cattle property in Western Australia, just beyond the Northern Territory border.*
>
> *Overhead flew kite hawks; outside the whitewashed boundary rock walls the plains stretched away, in nearby paddocks camels grazed.*
>
> *The day was well on its way. The goat girl had done her milking; the old gins had set off long before to winnow spinifex seeds for horse fodder. Across in the laundry native girls were doing the washing. Others were heating flatirons over a wood fire, or raking the paths free of leaves with bamboo brooms.*

Now smoko was over and the group dispersed. Mechanic, Arthur Renfrey, returned to his workshop. English Jean Langdon, the bookkeeper, went back to the station store. Governess, Rosemary Morrow saying 'Time for lessons', collected pupils, Jennifer (8) Randall (6) and, Lawrence (4) and headed for the schoolroom with its desks and black board.

And Mary Jones, picking up her six month old daughter Terri Lorraine, crossed to the kitchen where she could prepare for the 11.30 a.m. lunch while Terri slept in a cot nearby.

It was at smoko that the discomforting joke was so often repeated among station men.

'I like my tea like I like my women, black, strong and sweet.'

The men would laugh and the women smile with their mouths only. I felt very uncomfortable the first time I heard it and the discomfort stayed with me always.

I walked away from smoko without stacking the cups and saucers or carrying them to the kitchen. I was embarrassed because this was done by Aboriginal women twice my age. From somewhere I had internalised respect for Aborigines. I was not comfortable.

I went back to my quarters and changed all the furniture around and decided that later I would paint my bedroom. My bed had been made and the floor swept. I decided that in future I would make my bed and sweep up as I got up.

At 11.30 the wash-up gong went, work stopped and those of us eating in the homestead dining room, cleaned up. At 12.00 pm we went to the living room downstairs in the homestead. As I entered the scullery I saw a small boy pulling the rope near the pillar. The rope now had a use. It was connected to the punkas, big flat flexible sheets, which hung over our dining room table. The boy pulled our 'air conditioner', the punka, which as it moved stirred the air over the table.

'How much is that little boy paid?' I asked Stan.

'He's paid 6d. a week to pull the rope at lunchtimes and the boys change each week.'

We all moved into the dining room. There was roast beef for lunch, tinned peas and potatoes, and custard afterwards. Again the Aboriginal women did everything. We only touched our knives and forks and raised the water glasses to our mouths. The air was very dry, the sun very hot and the blowflies buzzed frantically and insistently on the fly wire wall.

After lunch we had a short rest and work began again at 1.30p.m.

That first afternoon I spent with the children. We talked about their interests, which were riding horses and chopping wood for Laurence, and working the forge and machine shop for Randall. Jenny, the eldest, was starting her first lessons in station cooking in the big kitchen. Gender lines were clearly drawn on the station.

Together we walked around the homestead area and the outbuildings again and I saw the trees they liked to climb, and their horses.

'This tree is good, because you can climb right to the top and see way out across the paddocks,' said Jenny. At the nearby horse night paddock I saw their horses.

'Mine is a black gelding and Jenny's is a bay mare,' said Randall as we came to the night horse paddock. It was very hot. I suggested we go down to the creek.

'Oh no,' said Randall, 'the Blacks live down there'. It occurred to me that I didn't know where the Aboriginal men and women lived.

'Can't we go and visit them?'

'No, we're not allowed down there'.

During the somnolent afternoon, I looked at the correspondence lessons, which came by plane once a month from the W.A. Department of Education in Perth. It looked pretty easy. I changed the room around and then had a sleep. As I drifted off I heard the KARK, KARK, KARK of the resident hopeful crows.

In the late afternoon everyone revitalised. Just before the dressing bell gong, stockmen hung around their dining room, rolled cigarettes and yarned with Henry. The cooks were busy with dinner and making the bread for tomorrow. Two men were chopping wood.

At 5.30 pm the first gong went and that meant we, of the manager's dining room, must all shower and change for dinner. Dressing for dinner was very important. Then, all scrubbed and in fresh clothes, we walked across to the living room and waited for Stan and Mary before entering the dining room. Dinner was cold roast beef, tinned beetroot and pineapple, followed by tinned peaches and homemade ice-cream made from powdered milk.

We ate quite badly really - all meat and tinned food relieved by fresh fruit or vegetables only for a few days each month after the mail plane came. There were a variety of recipes and none were very good. Curries were bland and boring. Roasts were roasts and were either burned or tough, or 'a good killer this time'.

After dinner we returned to the living room and talked. Again, the conversation turned on horses, cooking for tomorrow, rain and grass, cattle health, and the foibles of the Aborigines. The children were told that school would start with me in the morning. Mary took them upstairs to bed. At about 8.00 pm we all left for our separate quarters.

I stood outside my quarters and stared at the sky, the golden sliver of moon, the clouds building up in the north. I took off my sandals and stood on the cool grass, I breathed in deeply and smelled the dryness of the air and the moisture of the dew. A frog was croaking up more rain. The electricity generator kept a steady beat in its shed. An animal lowed and stirred somewhere.

Then that night drifting to sleep I detected new sounds. I got up, went outside and listened. Down beside the creek the Aborigines were dancing corroborees. Every night during the time I was at Gordon Downs I went to sleep to the sound of the corroborree. Those wonderful rhythms moved into my blood and bones and became part of my being forever. I loved the place and all the people passionately. I knew I never wanted to live anywhere else in the world in the whole of my life.

Defiant servitude

I looked down the 100 metres gentle slope to the creek and I saw a muddle of rusty corrugated iron, old timber and branches all tacked together like card houses. It was very dusty and there was no water. I saw some laughing children and many thin sick-looking dogs.

One hundred and twenty to a hundred and thirty Aboriginal people, elderly, young and middle aged, and many children lived down there. They lived there on the rations given to them by the station staff. There was one tap for water near the forge outside the white homestead fence, and every day women and children carried buckets down to the creek. The earth was bare, worn out by feet. They came to the homestead when summoned by the gong to collect their rations or to work. Only a few were allowed inside the white fence and green lawn. No children were allowed. Children, and even some adults, stood at the gates and called if they wanted to speak to one of the Aboriginal people who worked inside the fence. Most of the children had flies in their eyes, coughs, and yellow bubbles of pus from their noses.

The adult men and women had different jobs. At twelve or thirteen years old the boys were started as stockmen. The older men mowed and watered the lawn and some chopped wood. The women cleaned the homestead, my schoolhouse, washed, cooked, waited, and fetched tennis balls when we played tennis.

My gut feelings were strong. I hated it when Nancy cleaned my room and the classroom and I always tried to clean it before she came or simply worked with her and yarned.

But I couldn't think that white stockmen grabbing Aboriginal land was wrong. A year or so ago, I had been writing essays about 'the British taking possession of Australia', and 'brave explorers who rode out and claimed huge properties for sheep and cattle'. This was the heroic Australian history I had just finished learning. But I responded with numbness, not admiration, to stories of the Durack family droving mobs of cattle from Queensland to take up this land.

Understanding the impact on Aborigines of dispossession was easier because I had never seen people so poor and so ill. I also saw that the Aboriginal people had been brought to servitude and dependence through the forced occupation of their land. But I wasn't politically aware of the implications of granting ownership of huge slabs of Australia; of sensitive beautiful country, to be grazed to a dustbowl to make more money for Lord Vestey in London. This took a while to understand.

The Aborigines were issued with 'rations'. They were basically the same foods that we ate, except the varieties and quantities were different. Workers and non-workers received different allowances. I don't remember very clearly who received what. Station workers presented a flour bag for tea, sugar, beef and bread or flour. They were issued with no fruit or vegetables at all. I don't remember how the elderly people or children's rations were calculated, or whether they received any at all. Anyone could buy tins of jam or fruit from the store but these were not issued. I now realise that the Aborigines were supplementing their poor diets through hunting and gathering. This probably helped them retain some reasonable health.

Adult men and women were issued chewing tobacco, or 'makings' – papers, tobacco and matches – on a hierarchical system. Older and good stockmen received 'makings' whereas homestead gins got chewing tobacco. Older men and women nearly all had a wad tucked in one cheek and they spat constantly – a long, strong drizzle of brown yellow spit. The wad could be swung from one cheek to another. If a woman with a chewing wad was working in the house, she took out the wad and parked it behind one ear or over the door until she went outside again.

Stockmen on the other hand smoked a limp thin hand-rolled cigarette with the wet end of the paper stuck together and then stuck to the lower lip. This too could be swung from the right to left-hand side of the lower lip without touching it with their hands. Usually the tendency was to have the cigarette characteristically to one side so the smoke drifted up into the eye, which had to be closed. So with the cigarette and squint, faces were often unsymmetrical. The ordinary ringers usually rolled their own. So did I and although I got quite good at it, I also had a cigarette rolling machine; a small metal tin into which I placed the cigarette paper, then filled it carefully with the right amount of tobacco, and shut the lid. It spat out a cigarette and all I had to do was to lick the paper.

Only the whites sometimes had 'ready mades'. The blacks used to ask me for them when I had them.

The black stockmen were paid £2 a month and the women £1 a month (I received £10 a month). From this they bought material to make dresses, extra tobacco, soap, cottons, needles, extra food, and items for their children. Usually they bought on tick during the month before they were paid and so received no cash at all when payday came. Men managed to save a little more money than women did and when they were paid, they then played cards and the money went around. Sometimes shirts and boots were put up as stakes and often the card pack consisted of 45 or 47 cards. It didn't seem to make any difference to the enjoyment of the game.

None of the women and few of the men could write. None of the children went to school and everyone signed with a cross for their purchases and wages.

Soon after I arrived I wrote in a letter home:

> *Three tribes are employed here, making altogether, I guess, about 70-80 adults and about 30 picaninnies. There are laundry girls, kitchen girls, serving girls, and house girls. The men are stockmen, garden boys for the immediate house and those for the vegetable garden. Some have been to Darwin, Derby and Perth and can drive and others know a little about carpentry and mechanics but they are extremely lazy and have no idea of organisation.*
>
> *They speak in their mother-tongues and it is lucky that Jenny and Randall can speak it for they can tell the 'Boss' or Mrs Jones whether the natives intend doing as they have been told. Something else, which I should think is quite unique is that one of the tribes is fair. By that I mean they all have blonde hair.*

It sank into me slowly that the station cultural mores determined that they were THEY and not US. Distinctions were made by hierarchies. Also many comments and always some grievances endeavoured to instil in me and others that the Aborigines were inferior.

'You know what they did today....?'
'Someone.............

put hot wood on the fire and the bread, or roast had burned,
put cool wood on the fire and so the bread wasn't cooked,
hadn't chopped any wood,

hadn't pumped up the water,
put all the sheets on the beds outside the blankets last night,
put the wrong saddles, bridles, saddlecloths on the wrong horses,
brought up the wrong horses for the muster,
had spiked the tennis court,
put the wrong oil in the generator,' and so on.

Everyday there was another new and often wonderfully original sin committed.

This complaint was accompanied by head shaking and if possible one-upping the story. It was decided that they were thick and unteachable. Often there was anger -

'Because I told them so clearly, or

'I told them yesterday not to...'

Every night there was a corroborree down the creek and I remember the shrieks of laughter and joy accompanying some of the improvised dances.

Years later in Lesotho in Africa, I lived with the Basotho in their part of town, and during the day, at work I'd hear the whites discussing the Basotho in almost the same terms as I had heard on Gordon Downs. THEY, the Basotho and their capacity and what they did or did not understand. In Lesotho I lived in a totally black neighbourhood and at night I'd join with the locals as they told of the deliberate frustrations they had caused in their offices and work places. Again they would laugh till their sides ached.

I wrote in a letter home:

> *'Thieving is an everyday affair. I think their motto is 'Get what you can while you can', because a*

> *few of my things haven't returned from the laundry and the cutlery disappears from the dining room like magic. They break the blade near the handle and use them, when razor sharp, to fasten onto their spears.*
>
> *They consider everything as a big joke – one of the kitchen girls dropped a glass slab and two cakes on the cement floor. The cook was raging and swearing in German when she pointed to herself and said,*
>
> *'Me, silly bugger, no brains'. Then she and the rest of the girls went into hysterics which doubled them in two.'*

I realise now that what I saw on Gordon Downs was a quite deliberate long-term battle by the Aborigines, of non-compliance and disobedience in response to dispossession. They practised the techniques of the powerless. Some Aboriginal people were questioning their conditions.

I heard station managers and head stockmen, and the 'company men' talk about some Aboriginal men and women. I heard the talk at smoko, or meals but never over the radio.

'He's a bad bloody blackfella,' they'd say.

'She's a trouble maker.'

'Too right she is. Always talking about low wages and long hours.'

'What do they expect?'

'Don't let that Tommy on to your place, he's a right stirrer. Tells the others they are badly done by.'

'Yairs, I'll hunt him off straight away. He won't even get to the camp.'

'Yairs, good. Can't trust him and you don't need that type here.'

'OK thanks, so long.'

'So long.'

It was wonderful to me to see the Aborigines talk silently. They had a complete vocabulary of hand and head movements. They needed them of course to talk while tracking animals. It wasn't simply a matter of body behaviour, it was an information code. Nancy could tell us to 'come, go, stay, drop down, stand up, and move left or right,' and there were signs for hunger, sleep, and fine nuances for all the animals heard or in sight. Around the homestead, I'd look up and see Nancy 'talking' to her daughter outside the fence. I'd also see her 'talk' behind Mary's back in the kitchen.

I'd see the piccaninnies sometimes. They would follow, or track us down the creek, and watch from a distance. We never included them because of the ban on it.

'They were dirty, smelly etc,' They were. I contracted severe diarrhoea several times and evidently they would have as well. But for some reason it appeared as if only whites ever got diarrhoea.

The Aboriginal children at Gordon Downs did not go to school. They were not included in my small class because Stan said that the station owners did not want to explain the children's absences to the Education Department when their families went on 'walkabout' to check on their land and see it was in good shape. It sat uneasily with me because the children grew up illiterate in their own language and locked out of English.

I knew that I wanted to know lots about what they knew. I wanted to know the stories and history of the land, the animals and how to live up here in the Kimberleys. I realised I couldn't do it openly.

The pattern and rhythm of our days

The 5.30 am gong for the men's dining room and for me to dress woke me. I jumped up, washed, dressed and ran through the big kitchen, saying 'Good morning Henry' to the cook. He was having his morning milk – from tinned powdered milk. He gave me a wave as he turned the steak and I went to the dining room just before the second gong. The same breakfast steak and onions, toast and the same jams as yesterday with the wonderful hot tea.

I loved the stockyards. Many days I woke at dawn and made my way down to the yards. I spent hours perched on the top rail just at dawn watching horses being broken in the round yard, and watching the jackaroo learn to break horses. The morning was so quiet, the air so fresh and slightly cool that I felt rested.

A question asked of an innocent newcomer was:

'Can ya ride?'

If the answer was 'Yair' then the men would saddle the wildest, least broken, uncontrollable horse and put the newcomer on it, and invariably he was thrown. The correct answer, even for an expert rider was 'nar, not really', and this was said by men who had been born in the saddle.

Our communications with the outside world were through the two-way radio. There were scheduled times at 7.00am and 11.30am and 3.30pm. They were called scheds. The first sched for the day was the most important because this was when we picked up our telegrams and made appointments to speak to people on other stations. Every station had a call sign and ours was SQ and our base contact for the east Kimberleys was the transmitter called VJF Wyndham. Stations from the west Kimberleys called in to the transmitter, VJB, in Derby.

Just before each sched, stations would start calling in informally to make appointments to talk to each other privately at another time. Some people were known to write down these times and then listen in. This wasn't done at the stations where I worked, but everyone could name people who did.

There was competition for the airspace. Calls came from Balgo Mission, Flora Downs, Texas Downs, Nicholson, Sturt Creek and others. A good sched depended on the weather. In the dry season we could usually hear one another but in the wet sometimes we could not even pick up VJF. In the afternoons too the static was often too bad to receive Wyndham.

The operator in Wyndham would start by asking for urgent medical cases. If they were serious then he phoned the Wyndham base hospital and put the doctor on air. If necessary the flying doctor plane was called out. Most medical cases were accidents from horses or machinery. Everyone heard everyone else's messages and news.

At one stage, one of the Aboriginal 'boys' who was very highly respected developed specific symptoms which Mary didn't want to say on air and cause him to be ridiculed.

‘SQ, SQ to VJF Wyndham, good morning, can I speak to the doctor please?’

‘VJF to SQ, yes, can you give me some idea of the symptoms?’

‘SQ, well, um, yes, um, it is a male Aboriginal man of about 35 years and he hasn’t been very well for two days.’

‘SQ can you be more specific please?’

‘Well, he can’t urinate.’

‘Can you give more information please SQ?’

And, knowing the whole of the East Kimberleys was listening, Mary burst out ‘Well, his penis is blocked.’

The flying doctor plane came out immediately.

After the medical call, the operator went on to telegrams. He would say:

‘SQ, SQ, come in please SQ, over.’

‘SQ to VJF Wyndham, over,’ I would reply.

‘I have three telegrams for you, SQ, over,’ and he would read the ‘private’ telegrams over the air to all the ears who would then relay their details to others over lunch or smoko. We all knew each other’s personal and business affairs, despite family, friends and colleagues being asked to be circumspect in their messages. There were often indiscretions.

We learned which children were misbehaving for grandma, running away from boarding school in Perth, or were outstanding achievers. And we knew who was coming to visit.

We listened to telegrams about bank balances, family sicknesses, ordering booze, sackings from jobs and other information, personal, profound and trivial.

However, finally people just talked to break the loneliness. They used words as comfort.

They talked about how many points of rain and whether a cyclone was imminent.

One conversation I heard before a sched was among three women.

'We live here. We give birth to your children. We love them and nurture them, and then when they are eight or twelve years old, we send them away. We send them 2000 miles away to Perth to live at a boarding school, or to live with a sister. They come home once a year for six weeks. Then we all holiday, and the times are special but the relationships are artificial for such a short time. Why do we do it?'

'Yes, dear, it is like many small deaths, and we lose the joy of bringing up our own children.'

In the mornings, the children joined me in the schoolroom. We opened our books and began. I had checked what work had to be completed for them to be ready for the next plane in a few weeks time. I now know some of my ideas were beyond the children's ability but we muddled through.

Jenny was a mature, lovely child. She often helped in the kitchen and when she was eight years old, I heard Stan say, 'She should be able to cook a roast dinner for twelve people on the wood stove by now.'

Randall had little interest in anything in the schoolroom and passionately interested in everything outside it. He loved the forge and the machine shop and everything mechanical. He too was a good child on the whole and if I had known how to do it, I would have taught him everything he needed to know through his interests.

He had his moments in our time together, as this excerpt from my letter home describes:

> *Well its just 9.30 and everyone is in bed. I was out of bed last Monday – very weak but thrilled to be better. I've certainly been quite ill and weigh just 6 stone 8 lbs by the scales at the store. School started last Tuesday with Jenny only, as Randall was in Derby with his mother and the baby. Jenny is a delight to teach and this is the first job that I have ever got a thrill from. Randall and Mrs Jones returned yesterday and Stan (Jones) had to drive into Halls Creek a mere matter of 112 miles each way to pick them up.*
>
> *Randall was in class today and BROTHER was he plenty big mob o' trouble. He refused to come into the class to start – then refused to work, He stood on the desk and tried to kick me, then tried to throw a glass of water on me. Then four-year old Lawrence came in and didn't help things by riding his tricycle round the room. It would have put St. Trinian's to shame – needless to say there wasn't much work done.*

I was finding it increasingly difficult to teach the children because I was so distracted by the outdoors and the lives of the Aborigines. So we had more nature study lessons than the timetable ever scheduled. I would say, 'We'd better go outside now and see what's happening down the creek.'

We would wander off down the creek looking for honey ants, sometimes asking Nancy (who was becoming my friend) to come with us. She'd show us how to track our footprints and identify animals that had come to drink at waterholes. There were snakes, lizards, big roos, and euros. We could spend hours mucking around at waterholes. The days were hot and lazy, the stones warming and water cool. The children would float bark, look for birds, make dams and paddle. The sand down to the water holes was dry and dusty and we'd take off our sandals and drift our feet through it. I liked to lie flat on the warm sand and let the warmth seep into my skin. The dry eucalypt leaves split and smelt of oils.

I used to try to walk silently without letting a leaf crackle. It is very difficult and to this day, in bare feet or shoes, I can't do it. I'd walk on sand or rock with some success but the normal leaf litter is just far too noisy altogether. I learned a little tracking and I also learned how to watch and listen in the bush. When I did this an uninhabited place would suddenly become inhabited. I saw lizards, a variety of ants, birds sitting watching me, a grasshopper that had been invisible. I learned to scan the sky for a change in weather and to feel the different winds – cooler or hotter – on my cheek. I still report on small weather changes during the day to my friends.

However it would be years later that a friend from Cummeragunja, Rochelle Patten, really taught me about animals. We were walking past a house on 'Cummera' and Rochelle turned around swiftly and said angrily to a dog, 'Stop lookin' at me,' then turning to me she said, 'Animals really look at you and know you.'

From then on I practised 'looking at animals'. I'd see a magpie hopping along and then I would turn and look at her and say, 'Hello maggie'. I knew then that she knew me. I was part of her territory and accepted. The same happened with even small lizards – once looked at quite deeply and seen they knew you. The small finches foraging along the side of the house knew me and were quite confident only a few feet away.

The rhythm of our days was broken by special events.

Mail day was one of the most exciting. The monthly arrival of the MacRobertson Miller Airlines planes, locally known as Mickey Mouse Airlines, kept us busy writing letters 'home' for two or three days before its arrival. I wrote to Sydney, and others wrote to Perth or Brisbane. The plane came from Perth via Derby with the mail, and sometimes fruit. Usually Stan or Mary, the children and I went to the dusty cleared strip of ground to ensure that there were no cattle or 'roos on the strip, checked the air sock and then waited, scanning the skies for the tiny DC3 which emerged like a little insect out of nothing and nowhere. We helped the pilot unload the mail bags and bulky packets and parcels just like a monthly Christmas. We gave him letters and parcels to take to friends on other stations.

Back at the homestead, after the mail was sorted, each of us settled into chairs in a secluded nook, read uninterruptedly and were nourished by news from home. It was terrible to receive no letters. Often there was good news to share, and sometimes private griefs. Then we reached for the newspapers and magazines. For the next few days we had these to discuss.

My mother wrote every week on blue airmail letters. They were charming letters in the style of Jane Austen, with anything dramatic happening at home not described, but hinted at offstage. Terry was home. Sid had gone to back to Darwin. Mum sat at her ever faithful Singer sewing machine and made me really lovely clothes. She sent a beautiful little white linen suit, and some lovely orange and bright yellow long walking shorts and matching shirts. She must have put in hours and hours, thinking about me and making me these clothes. I really didn't think about her at all or what she was going through.

> *Rowie Darling,*
>
> *I'm writing this on my knee here in front of the fire, which will explain why my writing is worse than usual. Thank you for ringing Sunday night, it must have cost you plenty especially ringing Sidney. What were you doing in Hall's Creek? Don't forget Terry's birthday on Thursday – lst. We have sent him a good quality white shirt, long white sox, a navy T shirt with collar – most appropriate for our beachcomber I thought.*
>
> *I'm sending the review of 'A Nation of Trees' because I felt it might even have been a description of some of your experiences.*
>
> *Love from us all, darling, your Mum, the little ostrich.*

The most exciting items we received were the mail order catalogues. We poured over pictures of riding boots, shirts and stock gear from RM Williams. Then Mary, Jean and I went through the Boan's catalogue from Perth. There were fabrics, underclothes, summer dresses, cardigans, shorts, sandals and other women's necessities. We filled in the forms and waited. Sometimes there were grievous disappointments when the picture in the catalogue and the newly arrived item seemed to have no resemblance to each other at all. Sometimes clothes simply didn't fit. Rarely was joy and delight complete. I bought my ball gown for the Hall's Creek Races Ball from Boans and I was unhappy in it all night.

And, once every six months we sat together with the head stockman and composed our 'loading' lists. These were the shopping lists that we compiled for the whole station and included every item we thought we would need for the next six months. There was flour, rice, tea, coffee, jam, honey, butter and every other foodstuff for cooking. All the tools, nails, glues, saddler's implements, horseshoe nails, fencing materials, paints and building equipment that 150 people would need for half a year. Inevitably we forgot something.

Then about two months after despatching our order to the agent in Darwin, who then placed separate orders with firms in Perth, we would hear that the ship with our 'loading' on it had arrived in Wyndham. From the Wyndham docks it would be loaded on to two enormous trucks owned by two young men, Bob Wainwright and Wills, and then driven non-stop down to Gordon Downs. If we knew exactly when they left Wyndham, then a day later we would start listening in the night for the sound of the truck engines, which our ears could pick up four hours away. Then finally and still in darkness we heard the trucks arrive and we knew the drivers would throw their swags on the load, sleep, wake and have breakfast with us in the morning.

We all helped with the unloading and checking off the stores. After lunch and the recounting of the Wyndham and road gossip the truckies left again, and I was as disappointed as the children to have to return to the classroom.

I slowly grew more at ease with the people who were my employers, elders, friends, shopkeeper, paymaster and pupils. I also began making friends with the Aboriginal people although I intuitively kept this less visible. The station routine became familiar and normal.

I had recognised early, even if not consciously, that Stan was not only the manager of the station but that he directed the family activities. He visited the schoolroom, oversaw the children's after school activities and had a good deal of input into meals and recipes. My first interview with him when he briefed me on my duties showed me who I was accountable to.

It was Stan who decided that four-year-old Laurence would learn to ride and handle an axe to chop wood and who would teach him. It was Stan who sent six-year-old Randall to the forge to learn to start it up with the bellows and to learn work with iron. Stan naturally and easily managed everything. He did it well. I never saw him angry or domineering. I realise now he was fairly young, probably in his mid thirties. All things fell under his governance.

I was too young to notice the relationship between Mary and Stan but I sensed that Mary was not very happy. It could have been the isolation from family and friends. Terri Lorraine wasn't well and I wasn't proving a good teacher. She fed the baby Terri at the table and railed at the 'gins'. She spent the morning in the kitchen with two black women and Henry Ah Chin organising the meals for the homestead dining room, the stockmen's dining room and the blacks' 'rations'. After school the older children were allowed to run free and were safe, so they didn't require very much supervision.

Jean became a friend. She was an English migrant and still retained her accent. She was probably in her thirties and seemed very old to me. She had been employed from Sydney. She had quarters, a bedroom and bathroom, next to her office. Often in the evenings I would drift across there to chat in her office. She had suffered badly from acne and her face was scarred. She had beautiful brown eyes and a great sense of humour. She was always kind to me. In the evenings, Arthur, the bore mechanic was also there. He was 10-15 years older than Jean and I slowly realised that there was a love affair happening. Arthur was a quiet, dignified man who was well trusted in the Kimberleys and seemed to be able to fix any type of engine. He moved quietly and seemed to be always just where Jean was.

Being an in-between age, somewhere between adult and child, the adults didn't really talk to me seriously about many things that happened. Also some of it wasn't my business and anyway I knew so little about the life. So I observed some and missed some. However I was at all the meals and smokos where the conversation, after reviewing the weather, inevitably turned to discussing the Aborigines. I could also go anywhere – the men's dining room, stockyards, forge, meat house, kitchen, store and homestead. I wandered around this little village very freely.

The wet

I arrived in the wet with its red mud, gunship grey threatening clouds and terrifying storms. The paddocks were bright green and the grass grew fast and lank. The stock camp couldn't get out to muster and so there were lots of people at the station. They did maintenance jobs with horses, tackles, buildings, fences and mechanics.

The wet was cool because it rained. But between the storms the humidity would build up higher and higher and people would snap at each other like irritable dogs.

The mossies were savage. There were huge big ones that lived in dark wardrobes and under beds. When I opened my wardrobe they would fly out angrily attacking me. I always slept under a net. Sometimes one would get in and I would wake and find my bare arms stung hundreds of times in the soft skin of the elbow. Sometimes these bites got infected.

The stock camp went out for months in the dry season but in the wet season most men stayed around the station. Sunday was a holiday and the afternoons were fun. After a big lunch and sleep for some the stockmen, watched by me, would splice the ends of whips and ropes, and late in the afternoon everyone would go down to the stockyards. Everyone was me, the children and the men. The men would have rounded up young steers, put them through the crush and tied a rope around their necks. As they were released from the crush a man would drop onto the backs and then we'd have our own rodeo for the next few hours. The jackaroo took a lot of falls and even Randall would try a young calf and be thrown. Everyone got up laughing and usually limping.

Then we went back to the space near the men's quarters under the big peppercorn trees. Here we'd practice with stock whips – a cigarette whipped from your fingers, great precision but oh so painful if it stole a piece of skin. Then we'd walk on our hands. This was something I could do very well. So then we'd try hopping on one hand. This was really hard. I practised quite a lot behind my quarters. Legs wobbling in the air above my yellow shorts.

Finally we'd squat on our haunches in a circle, and they would yarn and I would listen with delight and appreciation. It was a story-telling culture.

'Do ya know about the mossies in Halls Creek? They're so big they'll remove the fly wire screens before they come and get ya. They take ya outside to eat ya and leave the bones.'

The men were kind to me and teased me. They were careful of their language and apologised for swearing in front of me. No one made a pass at me and I think now that I was very young and they didn't know how to approach me. I certainly would have choked if I tried to say hell or shit. I could say 'bloody' which was always explained as a contraction of 'by our Lady'. The men accepted me and included me in their practical jokes. And yet I didn't belong with them. Neither did I belong with the Jones family. I was somehow in-between everyone living on Gordon Downs.

One day Henry had been into Hall's Creek for a drinking binge. Everyone knew he'd return terribly drunk. Carefully they cut up a length of hose and took it over to his corrugated iron shed which was the cook's quarters, curled it up and placed it at the bottom of his bedclothes. It was exactly like a snake.

The generator was switched off. We all listened for Henry to come home. We heard the truck, then Henry bang the door to his quarters. A minute later there was the most almighty shouting and swearing and Henry came jumping out of his shed. Next morning, Henry was having his 'milk' as usual and only the head stockman said, 'Hear or see anythin' last night Henry?'

'Nup,' said Henry casually. I later learned that he always added a shot of rum to his morning milk – right against the station rules.

Henry later filled the stockmen's boots with molasses.

The cold dry

The green fluorescent grass gradually turned to bleached paper and crackled under foot. The landscape changed from green to gold then red. The dry season was with us.

In May or June the rains dried up completely until the next year. The last rains were scattered showers and we wouldn't see rain again for six months. The grass faded from green to yellow to bleached white. Many eucalypts dropped their leaves and made patterns on the ground.

And, at last, the nights grew cooler and then the days. I loved this season best. If there was no wind, the days were warm and the skies cloudless. Until the grass died there was no dust. I slept well at nights because it was cooler, and used a blanket. It was cosy at night. The nights sparkled and the stars were polished and shone proudly. I wore a pullover in the mornings and evenings. And shoes and sox, which felt heavy on my feet at first.

At night the universe gazed down benignly and the stars were crisp and sharp. I wish I had known that the Bushmen of the Kalahari say, 'You can hear the stars crackling if it is a quiet and clear enough night,' because I looked more than listened that first year. I was, and still am, comforted by infinity.

But there were also the winds, the unforgiving cold winds, which seemed to come from the heart of cold Australia in the south and chilled us to the bone. They carried dust, seeds, and actually seemed to cut through us. They were called the 'lazy winds' because they blew right through you. I remember feeling so miserable when these winds blew for days.

The hot dry

The weather grew even drier and hotter. Although the days weren't much longer, the sun rose high in the sky very fast and very hot. We moved our iron camp beds out under the trees in different corners of the garden and slung mosquito nets from branches and slept out under the stars to benefit from the slight coolness given off by the ground in the early dark hours of the morning. I needed skin and lip cream. My heels cracked open with little cracks even though I wore sandals.

The earth was pulverised by the feet of cattle and horses and dust raised from trucks and cars that were seen as little willy-willies. If there were two vehicles moving they had to travel far apart or the second driver couldn't see ahead through the dust.

It grew hotter and hotter. Grass shrank to little patches, some grew very tall, dry and empty then the red earth, compact and flat, encroached over the land and the waterholes dried up. Dust was in our noses and our teeth. We grew tired of it and dreamed of cool rain and green soft grass. We grew single minded and a bit desperate. Every evening we sat outside before dinner and stared at the north-western sky.

'A few clouds out there.'

'Too right, but nothing in them.'

'Might be.'

'Nah, it'll take a month for them to build up.'

'Wish it'd rain.'

'Yairs we really need it.'

Then one day someone would see a few scraps of white fluff in the sky.

'Hey, look, clouds,' they'd shout excitedly.

'That's only cotton.'

And from then on, we'd look to the north until we had cricks in our necks. And day by day the clouds would tentatively and teasingly come closer. We were obsessed by them.

'I reckon it'll rain tonight.'

'Bloody won't, not heavy enough.'

'Might.'

'Nar.'

The clouds coloured themselves blacker and blacker and bigger and bigger. I got a bit scared. Then the wet broke. The lightning raced around the sky. The horses raced in the paddocks. The dogs whined and tried to get inside. The cattle lowed uneasily. The rain fell in sheets and in the morning the roads and airstrip were closed off. The rivers ran red and broke their banks. And amazingly, the grass grew as we watched it. In three days it was six inches tall. The children and I measured it with our rulers.

At the beginning of the dry season the stock camp would go out for three months or more without returning to the station. They would brand and muster the cattle, which would then be driven on hoof for six weeks to the Wyndham meat works. It took a couple of days to prepare the stock camp. Horses had to be brought in – and there were five for each man. Stores were packed in the camel driven dray and the stock camp cook had to see he had enough food for several weeks. The men would live on damper cooked in the campfire oven. Food was very important and if the cook wasn't any good there would be a stock camp mutiny because it was one of the few things the men could complain about. Here the white ringers and the Aboriginal men ate around separate campfires. The white men had slightly better food than the blacks but basically it was steak and damper, jam and hot tea.

Ropes, whips, chaps, saddles, saddle blankets, shoeing tools, branding irons and swags were all checked and rechecked. Then the stock horses were driven in a mob out of the stockyards and on the road to the first camp. Around this camp the valleys, plains and river flats would be scoured for unbranded, clean-skin cattle, temporary yards built to earmark and brand them, then they would drove some back to the station.

The station was so huge there were few fences. Animals were held in mobs and temporary yards called bronco yards, which were really only a large right angle, were constructed. All the stock work was done on horseback. The man-horse teams mustered, cut-out, brought in, held back and headed off cattle. No one used dogs because the weather was too hot and the ground too stony for their paws. All the men were expert with stock whips. When the ringers were at the homestead they stood around in the evening making the new tails for their whips, and then practised plucking cigarette papers off the fence and other precision skills. They were always asking me to hold a cigarette in my finger and thumb and far out from my body and they would crack it. I never quite trusted them enough. While mustering and chasing the wild cattle they would swing the whips over their horses' heads and as they came to the rump of a bullock they'd sting them into changing direction.

Their other mustering tool was a rope. This was used to slow down the bull, or bullock, and then it was tightened while riding full gallop beside the beast, and as the animal slowed the ringer would drop off his horse as would another man, and they'd both drag the animal to a stop. Then a rope would be hooked around the animal's front legs and it would crash to the ground and the two or three men would drop on to it – twisting the head and readying the ear marking pliers and the branding iron.

Occasionally Stan spent days at the stock camp. He'd take mail and some extra food. Sometimes I went to the stock camp for the day but I wasn't allowed to stay. But it was what I really really wanted to do. I somehow felt ashamed that I couldn't. I knew it was because I was a girl. I never felt threatened by the men and my instincts about this were expert. I wish there had been equal opportunity regulations then.

Undercurrents

The rhythm of the days changed quickly when Stan was called to Darwin. Immediately Mary said, 'Let's have a party'. I wasn't quite sure what sort of a party because there were only us and they were all old – more than twenty-five at least. However she got on the radio and had OP rum and cartons of beer brought on the next mail plane.

The station, Stan had told me very clearly, was dry. That meant that no one was to bring or consume any alcohol on the station. Aborigines were wards of the state and weren't allowed to drink and somehow I thought the ban was because of them. Then I found out that there were others with alcohol problems. I got a bit nervous because Stan was strict and fair and wouldn't be happy about the alcohol. I didn't dare say I thought we shouldn't do this.

But it got sort of exciting that Friday night of the party. We, Jean and Arthur, Hans the German anthropologist from Bonn, Mary and myself, met after dinner in the homestead living room after the children had gone to bed. We put on records and danced a little. We started to drink.

'Oh yes,' I said confidently, 'I can drink. I'll have a beer please.' Having told everyone that I was eighteen, I had several beers. Mary and Hans sat drinking. We danced a little, then Jenny came downstairs so Jean said, 'Arthur and I are going over to my office, do you want to come Rosemary?'

' Of course I'd love to.'

We left Mary and Hans and strolled across under the stars. Once there however, the drinking became serious. Then Jean said, 'Have you ever tried OP rum and beer chasers?'

'Lots of times,' I lied – very blasé. I'd never heard of rum and beer chasers before.

I had three of these. They weren't easy to drink because the rum burned all the way down and then I had to drink the beer very fast. I felt strange.

'I think I'll go now,' I said, giving no sign of how dizzy I was feeling.

Later I found myself outside my quarters leaning against the walls and vomiting copiously and continuously into the garden bed. I remember looking up at the indigo night sky with its blue dwarf and red giant stars and finding them beautiful, before my stomach convulsed again and hoisted more rum and beer into the geraniums. I was so ill. The next morning I couldn't get up.

The drinking continued with the others for the next three days but now I felt allergic to alcohol and couldn't even think about it for a long time. Most of the homestead work stopped the week that Stan was away. Meals were late or cancelled, rations were cut short or doubled. The children started to give cheek and play up. I don't know if the head stockman and ringers continued their work but I now suspect that they were drinking as well. I knew that Stan would take this extremely seriously and wondered what would happen when he returned.

The day before his return a great clean up took place. Bottles were hidden or given to the blacks. Order returned. The kitchen and classroom became reliable and regular. But everyone who had been excluded from The Great Party, some stockman, the Aborigines, and saddlers, knew exactly what had gone on. I never knew Stan's reaction or what was said. Mary sometimes looked tearful but I wasn't sure. We were certainly subdued. Jean and Arthur were told they could not get married and go on living at Gordon Downs.

Gordon Downs was the heaven I'd dreamed of and yet I suffered a strange feeling of desolation. It was possibly culture shock and it puzzled me that I intensely loved the life but I had a huge pain in my heart. At nights I felt ill from the pain. It was barely tolerable. It may have been the adrenalin drop from escaping home and finding my dream. It felt like despair and I felt so alone. I wanted to be rescued and loved. I still don't know what it was about. I was so alone.

The anthropologist, Hans, was a bit like me. He didn't really know what he was doing or how to do it. As there wasn't a married head stockman he was given the head stockman's cottage. From this he carried out his studies of the 'tribe'. He would interview the Aboriginal men and women who spoke pidgin English. He would invite them to his quarters and ask them questions about tribal matters. After the interview the interviewee would come out with new sandals or shirt which I would see later tossed into the card circle as betting material.

As I grew to know Nancy and some of the Aboriginal men better they would talk to me.

'You know Missie, that fella he asks us big lotta questions. Then he ask us 'You fellas believe this eh?' and we agree with him. Bin make 'im happy that way eh?'

There was great hilarity as they agreed that they 'ate babies' or 'married their mothers' or whatever he put to them.

Hans earnestly discussed his findings with Stan and Arthur at the dinner table. Since very little was really known about the inner working and cultural life of the Aborigines, these conversations were further sources of misinformation for him and he realised that much of the information he was getting from the Aborigines was simply acquiescence or fabrication. He gleaned information from the stockmen and from visitors. But he was not there to get information from whites, who were often wrong in their knowledge or had made their experiences fit their theories.

He was a kind man, and although quite bald, he was probably only in his late twenties. Gradually the space, isolation and sense of his work not being quite right got to him.

He grew increasingly nervy and was especially irritated by the crows. Crows were everywhere. They cawed incessantly and it seemed, especially during the lunchtime nap. Mobs of them cawed at the empty sky from the coolibah trees. It was part of the landscape but Hans decided to stop it. It was like trying to stop a river flooding.

He made a cage with a wide door, baited it with a piece of steak and sat behind a tree trunk with a string in his hand holding the door open and waiting for the crows to enter after the bait. No crow ever entered. In the still, still, hot, hot days after lunch when we were dozing sweatily and uneasily, Hans sat behind the trunks of trees while willy-willies played on the ground and mirages formed on the horizon and the temperatures were 40°C+.

Hans grew dispirited. He never caught one crow. Eventually he quietly left the station.

However before he did he carried out one act of great kindness.

The family, Stan, Mary and all children, went to Derby because the baby was still whooping. She was thin and fretful and so they sought advice at a bigger hospital. While they were away I got dysentery. I vomited and had uncontrollable bloody diarrhoea. I couldn't move or clean myself up. I spent one day in filth in my quarters and then Hans arrived. He washed me, changed my clothes, picked me up and took me to the homestead to one of the children's bedrooms.

From then until I was well again, about five days later, he washed me, sat by the bed day and night, fed me liquids, washed my linen and carried me to the toilet. For a young single man to care as gently and beautifully as he did was a gracious and loving act. I have never forgotten Hans. He didn't belong in the exposed untamed spaces.

Before Hans left, Stan gave a party for him. We had Buddy Holly records and jiving. We had a wind-up gramophone and 78 records. There was no alcohol so we had fruit punch made with the juice of canned fruit, and cold tea and ice made in the kerosene-operated fridge. I was jiving with Hans and he swung me up then swung me down and dropped me on the smooth, red-painted, concrete floor. The pain was agonising.

'Hey, are you all right?' he asked.

' I'm fine,' I said but the pain was awful. To be in pain, sick or hurt was so feeble. I didn't want anyone to know so I stayed a bit longer then left early. I didn't know then but I had broken my coccyx. I hobbled around for a few days and it gradually got better. Nothing has ever been done about it but it made riding uncomfortable. It has remained misshapen and lovers later commented on it.

Perth had suffered a polio epidemic. One day there was discreet whispering among the station higher-uppers. I tried to find out but no one would tell me. The Aborigines were very quiet and seemed frightened. Several people were sick in their humpies down the creek. Then the landrover was brought out and taken to the creek and when it returned the back door was open and someone was lying in the back with their feet hanging out. Thin black ankles and paler soles of the feet. A grey woollen blanket covered the rest of the body. It was the first dead person I had ever seen. It was Rosie. They were going to bury her.

Stan started up the generator to power our two-way radio.

'SQ, SQ to VJF, Wyndham Base Radio,' called Mary.

The doctor was called to the radio base.

'Hello SQ, what is the matter?'

'I can't hear you very well Doctor, but we have had one lubra die here. She seemed to have symptoms like flu. No one from the camp told us she was ill.'

They discussed Rosie's death and decided it was the flu.

The police gave permission to bury her.

Rosie was buried immediately and a long way away.

That night there was keening and singing down the creek. The women cut themselves with sharp rocks and tore their clothes. The whole homestead became silent. Everyone, white or black, was exhausted and quiet. Except at night just after dark, when the keening began and went on until morning.

To break the atmosphere, Mary asked me to take the three older children to a waterhole for a picnic. We prepared the food the day before. We took salt beef from the meat house, some tinned tomatoes and fruit, and next morning we had fresh bread. We drove out to the waterhole with Willy, our driver, and had a lovely morning playing along its edges, looking under stones, climbing trees, and damming the water.

'Look a honey-ant's nest!' Randall showed it to me.

'And I've found a birds nest,' from Jenny.

'There have been cows and calves through here, and some horses,' said Lawrence, 'and there shouldn't be because Dad said this paddock has been mustered.'

'Well, let's have lunch. Collect some sticks and we'll light the fire and boil the billy,' I suggested. We ate lunch slowly and then we were sleepy in the still heat of early afternoon. As usual flies buzzed around.

I had crossed the creek and was lying on the dry grass and sand on the other side of the waterhole, when I saw Jenny pick up the billy from the fire. I nearly told her to put it down, but remembered this was the little girl who was already cooking roast dinners. I closed my eyes. Then I heard a splash and a scream. Jenny had slipped on a stone and the boiling water had spilt right up into the crook of her right arm. The skin on her arm was peeling off. Underneath the flesh was white.

I felt sick. I wrapped the wound, packed everything into the land rover and carried Jenny into the car. She was nearly hysterical with the pain. I held her as firmly and comfortingly as I could. I had no first aid. I was ill with guilt at having let her carry the billy, and sick for her pain. It was a long trip back to the station.

Eventually we arrived. Immediately Stan organised a mattress in the back of the Land rover. Mary, Terri Lorraine, and Jenny, now doped up on pain killers, left for the 110 mile trip over shocking roads to Hall's Creek where there was a base hospital staffed by nurses. I stayed behind to help Stan with Randall and Lawrence. Neither Stan nor Mary ever passed one word of blame or recrimination but I felt terrible and I still do because of the excruciating burn pain Jenny suffered.

When they came home after two days Jenny's arm was bandaged from shoulder to wrist and had to be dressed every day. Within another two days it was infected and suppurating. School stopped. Jenny's temperature soared, the glands under her armpit were up and the whole arm was oedematous. This time Stan asked me to go to Hall's Creek with her, back to the hospital. I felt so much better because they trusted me to go with her, and because I could do something for Jenny.

The hospital was a large generous open building, all fly wired with wide verandahs and situated somewhere behind the Hall's Creek Pub.

We stayed at the hospital, sharing a small ward at one end. There were two wards for Aboriginal patients, and their families lived in the dust at the end of the ward. They brought food to their patients and sat by the bed all day sometimes singing them back to health. They told stories and laughed.

Each day the nurses swabbed Jenny's large open wound and then pulled off all the bits of loose and infected skin with sterilised tweezers. Although Jenny had pain-killers before this, it was agonising. I held her and crooned sympathetic noises and tried to distract her but the pain was awful. I felt sure there was a better way to treat the burn than this torture. She was such a brave little girl and tried not to cry.

Then the wound started to heal. We went back to Gordon Downs. Stan ordered extra fruit to come by plane for Jenny. She was subdued and wan for a few weeks and then recovered but had to do special exercises so the wound wouldn't tighten the elbow skin and she wouldn't lose mobility of her arm.

Then I realised that Aboriginal children down at the camp also had burns from falling in the fire at night and suffered terrible pain, and their parents rubbed ashes, tobacco, or special fat on the wounds. Some children had burns that Mary treated by soaking in Condy's crystals or mild salt water. Some of their scars were incapacitating. Only the very serious cases were sent into Hall's Creek.

The Hall's Creek Races

Then mid-year in the middle of the dry season came the exciting time of the year that gave a crackle to our days. It was the Hall's Creek races. I was training a horse for the ladies race. Stan and the stockmen were training other horses. Every day I got up early and worked with Ginger – the ginger gelding that had been given to me. I loved the early morning but always suffered from a sense that, as I had learned to ride at the ripe old age of ten, I could never ever be a good rider. I was self-conscious about my posture, mouthing, seat and general horse handling. I wanted to be unselfconscious, totally free, wild and abandoned on horses and able to ride anything with four legs.

I loved the early morning light and riding, swinging in the stirrups of a jockey saddle. Standing, swinging, on a galloping horse was much easier and less stressful than riding in a stock saddle. Although I behaved confidently, I really didn't have much control of Ginger at all. He slowed down when he felt like it and when we came home, not because of any subtle hand and knee instructions of mine.

The men were eavesdropping on each other over the radio. They were making scheds to discuss horses, the races and performances. They spoke their special language of racing and times and distances and what horses and riders could do what.

All the women had received the Boan's catalogue from Perth and flipped through it endlessly before ordering race clothes. They needed day frocks for the races, then evening gear, and a ball gown for the Hall Creek Race Ball. It was the days of the ballerina dress and mine was truly horrible. It was nylon taffeta, strapless with big pink roses with green leaves on a white semi-transparent background. And I never felt comfortable in a strapless bra. I wore two petticoats and high heel white shoes, and felt like the doll on the top of the Christmas tree.

We wanted to be fashionable but we didn't know how. Ridiculously we ordered white gloves to go with the cotton dresses that we had selected, mainly shirtmakers, and now worried whether they would arrive on time and then whether they would fit.

With the difficulties of communication and distance, the Caulfield and Melbourne Cup fashions received much less attention than the Hall's Creek Cup.

We took the truck to Hall's Creek loaded up with the blacks. The women had made new shapeless dresses, the children in new clothes and the men in new stock gear. Everyone looked very smart. The homestead staff, like myself, went up in one landrover and Stan, Mary and in the children in another. I can't remember who was left at home to mind the million acres.

More than a week earlier our race-horses had been driven on hoof over the stock route to Hall's Creek and were now receiving extra rations to prepare them for their races. There were complicated arguments about what 'grass-fed' meant because horses were supposed to be grass-fed and not receive any grain.

We went to the Hall's Creek pub and booked in. Station hands were dropped off to make a camp at the race-track. Once the tents and flys were up and stores unloaded, the ringers made at once for the horse stalls and the track. Later, round the rails where the horses were stabled, I listened to the professional lingo of the ringers with a beer in hand, speaking in laconic monosyllables that could only be interpreted by experts.

'She's a goer.'
'Yairs, should do 200 in 20.'
'Yairs.'
'And the bay looks all right.'
'Yairs but fat.'
Silence for a while.
'Yairs.'

I couldn't tell from this which horses were likely to win but the men did. Stockmen didn't talk much. Their time spent alone on horseback, in camps, riding the mobs all night, or sitting with a mate they'd worked with for years, left them with few words.

They were scrubbed and shaven – at first. Boots were especially shiny and they wore light coloured moleskins with polished woven kangaroo skin belts and new cotton shirts with the folds still in. Some wore new hats. You could tell they were excited by the crowds and this big social event, because they walked with a bit of a swagger.

The whole town was as busy as King's Cross. Everyone had come. There were the managers from Flora Downs, Jimmy Klein from Texas, Sturt's Creek Station, Nicholson, Balgo River, Mabel River Downs and the Lilleys from Violet Vale. The one general department store was doing a fine business in everything from saddle needles to satin ribbon and the Pub bar

– Men Only – was packed with boasters discussing their chances. There was illicit betting behind the Pub.

The whole town consisted of the Hall's Creek Pub, the store, a post office, police station and lock-up, primary school, two churches, a hospital staffed by two nurses from Australian Inland Mission (AIM) and houses built of fibro on large dusty blocks opposite each other across a wide dirt road. There was a large Aboriginal camp. That was about it.

The races were scheduled for one weekend but the pre- and post- lasted one week. Stockmen and managers were known to go home after two days heavy drinking, sober up, then return to drink again for the last few days. It was on one of these returns to sober up that Alec Caporn, a ringer, stopped to make a fire, cook his dinner and drink some more. Some other ringers waited until he was in a stupor and then they earmarked him with the cattle earmarking shears of the Lazy W. Alec Caporn wore long hair before the Beatles.

The town looked crowded and integrated but actually consisted of four groups.

I don't know what the Aboriginal people did at the races but I suspect there was a lot of talk, gossip and corroborees. They were still considered state wards and were not allowed to vote, drink alcohol or be counted in census. As some tribes had been dispersed they met up here. Some must have had bad experiences from drunken whites, and some other scores that we would never know about would be settled under tribal laws. Also, the Aborigines were just beginning to become politicised. They knew they did most of the station work, that they were paid abysmally and were exploited and dispossessed. Whispers about strikes were just beginning to move from group to group from the western stations of the

Northern Territory to the west Kimberleys. Meetings like this one enabled a lot of ideas to be explored and passed on. I think it was like a large informal education centre.

The station stockmen came because they loved the horses, the racing and often just to drink. They consumed huge amounts of alcohol and some would pass out and others do things they would not want to remember. Some wanted to meet governesses, nurses and schoolteachers to find a wife, and some governesses, nurses and schoolteachers wanted to find a manager or head stockman for a husband.

The manager families were there to talk station and company business. Which Yanks or Japs were buying which stations, who was changing stations or retiring. This year they were discussing the impact of the introduction of road trains and whether they would be better than droving cattle to Wyndham abattoirs on the old stock routes.

'Nah, they'll bump the cattle to bruises on our roads.'
'Yair, they'll never replace the stockman and his horse.'
'Too right they will, they'll get 'em there fast.'

The white women formed another group, hungry for each other's company. They wanted just to talk to other women living in the same isolation as themselves. They wanted to talk about their children, the children's schooling.

'I'm worried about Elizabeth because she doesn't like living with my sister and then my sister says she is difficult. I don't know what to do.'

And the responsibility of station management as it fell to them. Very often the wives did the bookkeeping and taught the small children. Many did delicate embroidery, crochet, sewing or knitting. They swapped recipes. The offered each other TLC commiserating about the gins and their misdeeds, the heat, the lack of communications, separation from children, sometimes husbands who drank and medical problems. Their talk had flow, stroking and compassion.

'Poor Val, she has it really hard.'
'Did you know that ....'
'Isn't that so difficult when......'
'My mother has been ill and has no one in Perth......'

It wasn't the words – it was the tone.

The first day was 'settling in' day. Rob and Berryl Moody, still with English accents, were the monarchs of Hall's Creek, and owned and ran the pub. They knew every bit of Hall's Creek news and most of what happened on the stations. They were usually seated in cane chairs on the verandah and everyone staying there greeted them, swapped a few words and paid homage.

'G'day Tom, hello Berryl, how are ya? Hot isn't it?'
'What nag's going to win the Cup this year Tom?'

Tom Quilty and Olive Underwood came in from Springvale. They were a complicated couple because they had never married and had two sons. This was the first time I knew about it. And I had to think about this a bit. I watched them carefully. And there was another Quilty, Rod, from Tom's marriage. Tom had never been able to get a divorce from the wife, who lived in Brisbane, so he and Olive had lived together at Springvale and had the two sons. This was also new for me and I was very interested to find out that they had different surnames but the same parents. Their older son was Basil Underwood, and the younger one, Mick Quilty. Basil managed and lived on Bedford Downs station. Mick lived on

Springvale with Tom and Olive. Tom was widely known as Treacle Tom because of his meanness with his stockmen and Aboriginal staff. He fed them bread and treacle, and seldom enough so I heard when I listened to the women's talk. There were many, many part white-Aboriginal children on Springvale and Olive, who was gracious and kind, used to school them.

On Gordon Downs there were very few children of mixed white and Aboriginal ancestry. However I was aware, from oblique comments at morning tea and in the dining room, which stations did have large numbers of these children, such as Texas Downs, Bedford (many jokes about the 'bed' part of Bedford) and Springvale. There were not-so-subtle implications for what went on there. I knew it meant that many of these owners/managers were cheating on their wives. The wives knew and so did everyone else. There was an air of sympathy for the women for what they had to put up with and a feeling that the men's behaviour was a little contemptible. None of the wives left their husbands that I knew about. However Olive frequently went back to Brisbane for long breaks.

During these races Basil Underwood, who was 35 years old and in my eyes very old, wooed me. He asked me to dance and wanted me to walk under the full moon. I did find him attractive, but most of the attraction came from his being the owner of a very large cattle station and that meant the space, the stars, the dust, the horses, the cattle, the wonderful sunsets in the wet season and the excitement of cattle hunting in the Kimberleys. Marriage was really the only legitimate way I could belong to it. I imagined myself married to him and him visiting the Aboriginal camp when I was away, probably having his baby in Perth. Although I was only sixteen years old I knew that life with him would be no life at all. I kept my distance.

At the race-track each station put up a camp which was close to those of stations owned or managed by the same company. So Turner, Nicholson, Sturt Creek and Gordon Downs formed a little enclave. Although we were staying at the Pub, after dinner we went down to our camp. There the men drank beer and the women clustered and started some of the conversations that would continue for three days or more. I met some of the other governesses and we looked for the good-looking head stockmen or managers. We weren't interested in jackaroos because they were young and knew nothing anyway. We really would all have liked a manager or owner but there were very few who were eligible, and anyway I gathered that schoolteachers and nurses came before governesses so my confidence wasn't very high. Mick Quilty was eligible but he was only 21 and too much of a boy. We sort-of knew that Olive wanted him married pretty quickly, probably to keep him out of the Aboriginal camp.

The next day was race day, and I was to ride. I had never ridden in a race before but I had been training in the mornings for the Single Women's Race and the men had fed and groomed my horse for me. I was very nervous. There were only three of us in the race. At the start, Ginger took off and ran a really good race so I came second but at the end he didn't want to stop. He kept galloping and I couldn't pull him in. Finally we arrived at a fence when he stopped dead and I went over his head. His front hoof as he blocked, came down and took a chunk out of my head and removed the hair, but he didn't actually bruise my skull. Everyone cheered. I was so embarrassed that I shot away and hid. Someone collected Ginger and took him out of my sight. What had been unpleasant for me was nothing to the others who never even mentioned it because it was too trivial.

One of the most humiliating situations I have ever undergone occurred at lunch time. It was a tradition to auction off the single girls before their footrace. Men bought them and also placed bets on them. It was awful to be lifted on to the tea chest where everyone looked at your legs ... and the rest of course. I loathed it and them. However I looked athletic and had good legs so the bids were quite high and my secret satisfaction was that I had lots and lots of style ... I looked as if I could run like a cheetah ... but in reality I was as slow as a tortoise. And that's exactly what happened and men lost their money as I came last. I was never in any auction again. Once the race was over the other girls never ever mentioned the auction. It was the silence of shame.

The second night was the Race Ball. I wore a horrible creation bought from the mail order department of Boans. As usual I felt that my dress wasn't right. I had that feeling for years from the time I was about twelve. I later came to develop a style I felt good in. I think at that time there was no style which I would have felt comfortable in because I didn't really know who I was.

The Hall was huge and hot. Tables were laid outside for eating and drinking. We did the foxtrot, the Pride of Erin, the three step, the waltz, and others – a mixed cluster of romantic and family dances. The dust rose off the floor. Soon we couldn't see very well. My eyes were red from the dust. My shoes hurt like blazes because they were too tight, too high and my feet had swollen.

I danced with drunks, with sober men in riding boots, and with children excited about being up so late. Everyone was white.

Jimmy Klein from Texas Downs, had lived for years with Julia, known as the Yellow Rose of Texas. She had cooked his meals, shared his bed and kept him clean, but was not allowed, by unspoken rules, into the Hall.

The age demographics of the white community were quite skewed. There were almost no older men or women since most owners/ managers retired to the coast when they were in their mid-fifties. There were no children aged eight to twenty because they were being educated in Perth or elsewhere. So there were young children, their parents and us, the young adults of very mixed types and backgrounds.

The older women and mothers went off to bed quite early, telling us to come straight back to the Pub and not to stray away with any men. I danced with red-faced, very freckled, slightly fat, 35 years old (very old indeed) balding Basil from Bedford Downs. He was keen and clutched me close and smelt of cigarettes and stale alcohol. His fat stomach pushed against me. He wasn't a very good dancer. I pushed him away.

Except for those few who were looking for wives, most of the men got very drunk.

Many men from dry stations were secretly alcoholics and this was when they binged. They had bottles of rum, whisky and brandy – but mainly 35% OP Bundie rum to strengthen their beer. Some would be drunk for the whole week at the races.

The Aboriginal men cared for the horses, groomed them and kept the fire going at the racecourse. They were sober and extremely observant of the behaviour of their bosses.

One evening I was going to visit Maureen Lilly at the Bow River Station Camp when something pinged by my ear. I sprang back. Someone had fired a gun down the length of the one and only main street. There were more shots to follow and I hid in the shadows. No one came to see what was the matter or to stop the gunman. Eventually the firing stopped. Firing rifles down the main street was quite common.

Five days later the town was emptying. The dust blew across the roads and the spring seeped out of the visitors' step. A cold wind heavy with dust blew from the south. The stockmen and jackaroos were tired, hung over and crumpled. White shirts were stained with mud and blood. The horses stood around with their heads hanging down.

We went around the Aboriginal camps and found the stockmen, women and children. Fifty or sixty men, women and children crowded onto the back of our open truck. I went home in the landrover. Mary, Stan and the children went in their car. The big event of the year was over until next year.

Life with animals

Camels

There was quite a deal of talk which I didn't follow about the 'Ghans and the camel train. Then one day Bert, one of the Aboriginal stockmen, told Stan that the camel train was coming. I went outside to see but then Nancy told me that they were two days walk away. I asked Nancy more about the camel train.

'It's that old one, black man, 'Ghan im fella, with 'is camels. He bin come fixim up saddles.'

And that night at dinner Stan told me that, 'An old man, Afghan Alf, of mixed descent, mainly Afghan with some Aboriginal and European blood, travels with his camel team around the cattle stations that fringe the Tanami desert. He's been doing it for about fifty years. He travels with dogs and his large extended family and camps out in the desert. He hasn't been known to visit Derby, Halls Creek or Wyndham and he buys his stores from the stations.'

'How amazing that he still lives an Afghan life in the Australian desert,' I thought.

Then Stan went on: 'You know, Rosemary, that people catch syphilis from camels.'

I looked at everyone else at the table to see if they were smiling. I had to think about this one. I didn't know much but I did know the facts of life and this didn't make sense.

Late the next day as the sun was setting a huge ruby fireball in the western sky, through the golden haze beyond the stockyards I saw the dusty silhouettes of the camels. They lumbered and swayed as they came to the yards.

We all went down to see them. The camels opened their mouths wide then yawned bad breath over us and showed us their green slimy teeth. They drank gallons and gallons of water from the horse trough and then lay down with their front legs bending first – opposite to horses. That night, because some of Alf's relatives were related to the station Aborigines, there were shouts of laughter and then a very late corroboree. Evidently there was a lot of news being passed on. The camel train was also a verbal newspaper.

Straight after breakfast, first thing, we were all at the yards because we had been offered camel rides. Jenny, Randall and Lawrence had time off from school because this was an annual event. However the Aborigines were late coming to work. We climbed the stock rails and stared at the big dusty, matted-haired, plate-footed animals, so different from the horses we were used to riding.

I came in for a bit of teasing as the stockmen asked me: 'Hey, you know what diseases camels carry?'
'No, what?' I replied wide-eyed, wondering if they were game to say the word syphillis.
'You game to ride one?'
'Too right I am.' I was too.

Finally Alf turned up from his breakfast in the men's dining room and clicked, grunted and indicated by head and by hand that the camels should kneel down. They did. Then they were saddled and the rest of the day we spent with the stockmen learning to ride a walking, getting up, getting down and finally a trotting camel. It was magic and exhilarating. The younger Aboriginal and white stockmen stayed with us while Alf went shopping at the station store. I guessed he would resell the cheap printed materials, chewing tobacco and men's shirts to other Aboriginal tribespeople further out in the desert.

At the beginning of the dry season when the long green grasses were drying off, there was always anxiety about losing this feed, high in nutrients, to fire as it dried. So some men took camels, harnessed them and pulled a railway line along fences scraping away the grass and leaving bare soil so fire could be controlled. The camels made the firebreaks.

Breaking in camels was very exciting. They bit and kicked forwards because their front legs could bend forwards whereas horse's front legs cannot. A frightened and non-cooperative horse looked and behaved the way it felt but a camel could look quite calm and agreeable and then go quite mad striking out everywhere. They could also bite hard and deeply and some of them enjoyed biting. They were so unpredictable.

Camels, I realised, were animals that you either loved passionately or hated vehemently. All the stockmen not working far away that day hung over the rails intrigued by the differences.

I loved them and every afternoon after smoko I asked Bobby, one of the members of the camel train, to saddle up for me and I'd ride away into the dry distance. We'd walk out to a creek or billabong and then trot back gently. That one week in my life is more memorable than perhaps 584 others.

I have often wondered since then whether the camel train was carrying news from the Aborigines on other stations, questioning their dispossession and their treatment as partial slaves under humiliating conditions. At nights the corroborees had quite a different sound. I think the stories were different and the men and women painted themselves every afternoon for that night's dancing. The pace was faster and the laughter sharper.

Alf and his wives, several daughters and sons and others travelling with him only stayed about ten days and then they disappeared early one morning in single file with their backs to the sunrise. We didn't see them again that year. However I think one of the white stockmen got syphilis so it must have been the camels.

Goats

We also kept a herd of around 300 goats for their meat and dairy products. The nannies were brought in every morning and milked so we had fresh milk. The milk was separated by hand and the cream sat in the kero fridge for a couple of days. Then it was brought out, colouring and salt added, churned and patted into butter. This was infinitely better than the rancid tinned butter in the swollen tin, which came from Perth and was a nasty tasting oil by the time we used it.

On Saturday and Sunday mornings I used to go to the milking shed. I'd take a stool and squat behind the nannies and squirt milk into a billy. The kids were like pretty little puppies and scampered and jumped, sometimes with four legs off the ground at once.

I like the smell of them.

And we often killed goat for meat as a change from beef because we ate meat three times a day. Visitors who didn't know that there were no sheep at all in our area, would often compliment us on the delicious lamb. Others complimented us on our fresh dairy butter – but this certainly wasn't cow country.

However the goat flock was always diminishing even with the Aboriginal boys sent out as herd boys. Evidently the Aborigines, always hungry for fresh meat, found it easier and quieter to knock off a goat and hide the evidence than a bullock. Dingos were always blamed and the story was never believed so the manager always threatened.

'You'll all be run off here if I find out who did it.'

But, back to goats ... one billy who had been castrated at a rather mature age, was broken in and trained to pull a goat cart. One of the good things to do late in the cool of the afternoon was to harness the billy to the goat cart and drive out along Halls Creek road. I played games with the children and made up stories of running away and princes and princesses in goat carts.

Living with horses

A big round-up of horses took place twice a year. This was more exciting and faster than rounding-up cattle. The horses interested all of us, the homestead dwellers and the creek dwellers. We all loved these speedy, slender legged, wide-eyed creatures.

The station had about a herd of about 500 horses and most of these ran freely. However they also had to be managed. They were rounded up and brought to the homestead twice a year and all the foals were branded, the colts were castrated, and stallions were selected for breeding qualities and to ensure they could protect the herd from the predatory instincts of the wild brumbies. The two year olds had to be broken in and some would make stock horses and others pack horses.

The younglings ran free over plains with no fences for the first 18 months of their lives, watched over by the mares and a stallion. One stallion herded 30-50 brood mares and their young. The brumbies, the wild horses that had never been broken in, wanted to raid the station mobs and take away the mares. They hid in gorges at the desert edge and would challenge the stallions.

Once I was out mustering with some of the men when I saw two stallions fight. Suddenly Harry cried out, 'Look out Rosemary. Move away fast.'

I'd learned to obey orders like that.

'The stallion will try to bring your mare into the mob and will use his hooves to do it.'

I moved. I could imagine the cutting force of the front hooves.

We moved downwind and watched from a small hill.

When stallions fight everyone moves away. These muscle-bound males in their prime, trotted up with their ears flat to the heads, eyes wide, nostrils flaring and tails raised in a plume. The raised top lip showed huge yellow teeth. Then they screamed. The noise was different from a neigh or a whinny. They circled and assessed each other. Then came closer and closer. Rearing on his hind legs and with forelegs striking out, one came down on the other, which then turned his rump and lashed out a mighty kick with both back legs. The wounds were lacerating and bloody. Hoofs clashed on boney heads and against hoofs. If possible one stallion tried to sink putrid teeth into the flank of the other. The battle for mob supremacy continued for more than an hour.

Mares and foals watched from a distance. They were being fought over. The end came when each stallion stood off, clouded in red dust and then the beaten brumby would hobble off, to watch the mob from a distance until the day came when he was ready to contend again. The victor then trotted twice around the mob neighing, whinnying and bringing them tight together.

The stock horses were co-opted to work with men with whips and ropes to round up and bring the unbroken horses in. They could turn on a thruppence, and they cut out the stallion near the horse paddock so he didn't run in with his mob but waited anxious and fretting at the gate. The mares were then cut out from their foals. They were put in a small yard and checked for brands. Last year's gelded colts were separated out for breaking in as working horses.

It was shocking and traumatic for the foals brought in to the station. The new foals were herded to a small yard near a race. Here each one was bronco-roped and dropped to the ground and one stockman sat on its head, another held the ropes and a third had a knife ready for gelding. A small team of stockmen had the fire burning hotly and two or three of the station iron brands were already glowing red.

The foals screamed and struggled as the hot brands sizzled on their shoulder. Their mothers would answer anxiously. An experienced stockman would reach between the legs of the colts and make the smallest slit possible and then squeeze out and cut off the testicles – dab the cut with antiseptic, then hoist the testicles to the group of blacks who'd scramble to take these delicacies home for dinner.

When the ropes were released the young animal would lie silent and trembling then suddenly leap to its feet and push its way up the D-shaped crush to find its mother in the worried mob.

Breaking in two year olds was the young horse's next rite of passage and trauma.

The yearling was pushed into the round horse yard. I'd be perched on a top rail. A specialist breaker, Percy, stood in the centre with a long stock whip and rope, and with continuous talking and clicking encouraged the youngling to walk, trot and canter around the yard. Then by using the whip lightly on its flank and voice, he would bring it around to face him.

'Whoa, go, come on now, walk-up, steady goes it, quietly now,' in a steady monologue, the whip lazily rising and falling, behind or in front, teaching the horse which direction to move in.

Percy used old bread for a reward and his pockets were always full of it. The animal was loved for behaving the right way. It had to learn to approach Percy with his staring eyes, and be fondled, its nose rubbed and neck stroked, and patted all over. Percy became more and more intimate and still clicking, breathing into its nostrils, hands down the legs to the knees, lifting the hoofs, encouraging and soothing.

By the end of the first day the whip was like a halter around the yearling's neck and it was learning to walk with it. During the long hot lunch-time break the horse was left alone and without water. When Percy returned the sun was scorching and the man carried a bucket of water. He approached the horse, held the rope around its neck and encouraged it to drink. As it drank the horse was cooled and washed down. Now it would learn to accept the bridle.

The reins to this bridle were around twelve feet long and the breaker took the centre of the yard again. The horse was encouraged to walk, trot and canter with Percy teaching it mouth orders behind him. It tried to spit out the bridle, tossed its head, frothed at the mouth yet couldn't escape the signals from the man's hands. The reins could tighten and the bit would cut into its soft mouth.

Everyone was sleeping away the heat restlessly. From the fence where I perched, the gritty dust tasted dry in my mouth. I moved to get the sun on my back. My shirt armpits formed dark circles of sweat, and I felt dizzy from the heat. In the distance I saw a mirage of water and trees where there were none. I couldn't leave.

The horse followed instructions through its mouth via the bridle.

Over the next three days it would learn to carry a saddle, get used to the circingle tied tightly under its belly. It had to walk, trot, canter and gallop – then stop and turn with the bridle and saddle – and all these instructions from a man on the ground.

Then it had to learn to obey a man in the saddle through his knees and heels. Percy leaned over the saddle, put his weight on it five or six times, then suddenly dropped the stirrups and mounted. Now there were five or six of us watching. The horse would buck, toss and sometimes roll. We shouted and counted the seconds Percy stayed in the saddle.

Finally the gate to the round yard was opened and the man and horse, now a team, rode into the big horse paddock. It behaved well. Now its working life began as it learned to ride behind a mob of cattle, to cut out bullocks, to turn swiftly, to prop, and to shoulder cattle. And perhaps it would become a stockman's favourite and receive extra bread, sugar and praise.

Some horses enjoyed being part of a team. Others learned more slowly, and some objected all their lives to being broken in. These were the kickers, biters and buckers.

After a day's horse-breaking, during which almost everyone had watched, the white stockmen shaved, showered and changed for tea (we had dinner) and would come up across the green lawns and under the shelter of the big trees. They squatted on their toes, rolled their smokes and quietly yarned about breaking in horses. They allowed me into their circle. At these moments with the tropical sunset, cool dry smells from the soil, the world was quiet and at peace, and tranquillity descended.

In the kitchen Henry was swearing in a good-tempered way. The usual smell of wood smoke and roast meat drifted across to the creek. There the blacks were lighting their fires, cooking, chatting, calling to one another and forming kinship circles. Somewhere there the night's corroborree was being sketched out and the greatest hilarity was when the young horse nearly kicked the breaker in the groin.

Later just before the stock camp went out, horses had to be shod. Shoes were important because the ground was hard, stony and hot. Horses travelled fast and turned quickly, propping in mid gallop. Lameness was agonising for the horse because the frog was tender and a failed leg could kill a rider. Anyway horses seemed to like their shoes.

The forge was stacked with wood and the horses closed in the yard closest to the forge. The fire was started before dawn and the wood burned hot. The smithy had rows and rows of iron horseshoes (only racehorses had aluminium shoes for the Great Hall's Creek Races), all lined up by size swinging on a line of No. 6 wire, as befits a shoe shop. His shop had only two walls and the horses were haltered close to the forge in the open.

The smithy approached the horse's front legs with his back and then pushing hard with his back into the horse's chest, he pushed its weight back onto the other three legs. Then he picked up the front leg and held it between his knees. He cleaned out around the frog and seizing a huge rasp rasped smooth the broken and overgrown hoof. All this time he talked quietly and evenly to the horse – telling it what he was doing and why. It was a painless operation but some horses needed reassurance.

The smithy reached for two or three horseshoes and found one to fit, then with pincers he'd thrust it into the forge until it was translucent red hot. He hammered the shoe to fit the hoof. Someone else would pump the bellows to ensure the heat was maintained. The horseshoe was dropped sizzling and steaming into cold water and then cooled, it was placed on the hoof – really a huge fingernail. The smithy tapped it onto the hoof – taking the nails from his mouth and hammer from his leather apron.

This was done for the other three hoofs then the halter was taken off and the horse tapped lightly on the rump to tell it it was free. Off it would trot headed to open paddock – always lifting its newly shod feet high and delicately as if to show-off its brand new shoes.

I tried shoeing once but when I pushed back into the horse's chest it leaned on me and when I tried to hold the hoof in my left hand and the rasp in my right, I couldn't actually hold up the heavy iron rasp in one hand. The men laughed at me.

The saddler was itinerant and visited all the Vestey stations. He was booked by the two-way radio and then Stan would tell us at breakfast.

'Jack, the saddler, is coming and will be here about two weeks. He'll mend all the saddles, pack saddles, and camel and goat harness.'

The children and I were thrilled. We went over to the saddle shed with its stock saddles, racing saddles, pack saddles, and harnesses of all types. It was a dark shed and full of cobwebs. Each saddle hung on a large wooden rail out from the wall - about fifty of them. We used to climb up there and sit on them for fun sometimes.

Jack arrived in his old truck with a hand-operated sewing machine that had a huge strong needle and unpacked his equipment. Punch, leather thongs of various sizes, needles of many sizes, knives, scissors, hooks, bobbins and lots of other things I didn't know the name of. Jack sat cross-legged on a big wooden table on the verandah outside the saddle shed and sewed and hammered for a week. He told us stories.

And then cattle

If horses were the soul of station life then cattle were the heart. 10,000 head wandered one million acres. That's a low stocking rate and yet gradually whole patches of land became dustbowls. Stan sent some old gins out on quiet horses to collect sugar bags of grass-seed in the dry season to broadcast over the pounded earth in the wet season. The cattle lived along the waterholes, the creeks and the bores. Water was life. Keeping water up to the cattle was a major part of station work. Keeping the bores pumping was Arthur's job.

The cattle were mainly shorthorns. To belong to the station I had to learn the lifecycle and vocabulary of cattle – bulls, cows, steers, bullocks, weaners, two-year olds, heifers, calves, sucklings and cleanskins. Then there were the brands, for each animal was branded on the flank and every station had its own brand.

'I saw some lazy J steers out near Dead Horse billabong yesterdee.'

'Didja? Well I'd better tell Bill then.'

It wasn't supposed to be done but sometimes a cow branded for one station, would have its calf branded for another! This caused bad feeling between station managers.

The stockmen knew where the mobs hung out – which billabongs and grassy valleys. They knew also where the cattle raced away from humans to live wild and unbranded all their days. These were the cleanskins. There were hills and valleys in the north where the wild cattle hid out. If they succeeded for more than one generation the wild genes exerted themselves and these cattle could run very fast. Rounding them up required expert men, horses and whips.

It took a specialist eye to see a good animal. It had to have rounded flanks and be well covered. I got good at estimating the live weight and the dressed weight of bullocks. Years later in Queensland the farmers were impressed when I appraised their cattle. Some calves were selected to be future breeding bulls. They were selected for fertility and weight for age. I had to be really careful of these in the yards and it was a game to drop down the stockyard rails and cross in front of a bull then scamper up the rails as it chased me. It was just as dangerous in the crush if a friendly 2200 lb bull leaned on you up against the rails.

There was a cycle to the life of the cattle as there was for the horses. The cows were mated in the dry season and watched to ensure they had grass, water and safety at calving. Calving was in the early wet season when there was abundant grass. Then the calves were branded and most castrated. They were put out in the paddocks again until they were about two years old and able to walk to Wyndham. Some older cows were included in these mobs. Threats to calves came from the crows, which pecked the eyes out of weak calves, and dingoes also attacked the weak young. Station managers became enraged if meat-hungry Aborigines killed cattle, however it still happened and no one ever knew anything about it.

'Who Boss, kill'um bullock? No, no boy ever kill bullock Boss, no Boss, real scared fellah to kill'm.'

The cattle made the money. Several mobs of 800+ were driven on hoof up the stock route from Gordon Downs to Wyndham abattoirs. A trip of about six weeks and it was hell if the animals had to go more than two nights without water. The mob would rush the next waterhole and trample each other to death. The ringers had to cut out smaller mobs and hold back the parched animals until the first mob had drunk. Sometimes during the night hours when the men rode around the cattle singing, animals would break. The night watch had to get out in front and keep turning them in a circle until the others came to help.

At Wyndham meat works the animals were slaughtered and we used to go and watch the man-eating crocodiles, which lazed off the point waiting for the offal.

Mustering one million acres on horseback was a huge job. The station was divided into portions and periodically the mobs of cattle were rounded up way out, miles from the homestead and only those to go to Wyndham, or close to the homestead yards were brought in. But when they were in the yards the homestead sat in a haze of red dust. We gave up schoolwork, on any pretence anyway, and headed for the yard. Jenny and I hung on the gates to swing them open, or shouted to encourage them through the race. By smoko we were covered with red dust, even our eyebrows, and sweat beads hung around my hairline. We felt we had earned our smoko.

Winding up and winding down

I had been there through a wet season, a cool dry season and a hot dry season and I still thought it was the most perfect life for me. I couldn't imagine ever leaving it or wanting to live anywhere else. The pace was slow, the days quiet and the nights soothed my spirit. I loved each new day when I sat on the stock rails and watched the skills of man and animal against the landscape.

Gradually I got an understanding of the correspondence lessons, and the children were learning something. I thought I was handling the children's schoolwork quite well. Lawrence, now five years old, was supposed to be in class all day. I could manage Jenny and Randall but Lawrence was wild. He couldn't and wouldn't settle. Stan threatened him with beatings but he ignored them. He just wanted to play. But he was bored outside without Jenny and Randall to play with.

And, like the children, I preferred to be outside rather than inside. I hated keeping them inside when they wanted to be outdoors. I felt as if I were a brutal and mean person. I guess that intuitively I knew outdoors was best. We'd work through the reading, pothooks for writing, learning to count with coloured counters, and as soon as possible I'd say, 'Time for nature study children.' And we'd close our books and wander off down the creek.

Down the creek, whether it had water in it or not, was fascinating. Shoes off, and with Nancy or one of the other lubras to teach us, we'd start practising tracking.

'This way,' said Maggie, 'see you fellahs, that heel there, that's Billy goin' up to see how the honey ants are.'

'Let's go there then,' I'd say in my best teacher voice.

In file up the creek we walked carefully with bare feet on hot stones and crisp sand.

'Stop now,' said Maggie, 'be quiet and you'll see the big fella kangaroos sleepin' on the grass near that one water hole.'

Stopped, we looked until we could see the big reds lying on brown dry grass in the mottled shade of a coolabah. The children were much quieter than me and quicker at spotting the semi-camouflaged 'roos. They'd push their bottom lips out to the full and turn their heads, as the Aborigines did, to show where I should look.

We were all at ease standing for a considerable time on one leg with the other leg bent and the sole of the foot resting on the inside of the knee. We'd wait and watch, until the big old man red, growing uneasy from our gaze yet unable to see us, and with ears twitching, would chatter at the mob who'd slowly pull themselves up and lope away.

Next we'd make musical instruments with leaves, blow through them and try to reproduce the songs we sometimes played on the gramophone at night:

> *'Old Faithful, we've roamed the hills together,*
> *Old Faithful, in any kind of weather,*
> *When your round-up days are over*
> *There'll be pastures white with clover*
> *For you old faithful pal o' mine.*
> *Giddy yup old fella,*
> *Cos the moon is yella and bright*
> *Giddy yup old fella*
> *Cos we gotta get home tonight.....'*

And the music to 'Harry Dale The Drover', and 'The Old Black Billy', and the gloriously sad and sentimental songs of dead dogs, old horses and girls back home who either stayed true or went off with someone else. I've loved country and western music ever since.

Next we'd look for water to drink. Squatting on our haunches we'd dig deeply through the river washed sand until we tapped into the underground stream. Then lying on our bellies we'd lean over, cup our hands and drink from the small soaks we made.

'Come on then,' said Maggie, 'we gotta find some yams and witchetty grubs.' For her, this was a serious supplement to her station supplied rations. For us, well, it was nature study.

'Now find a stick about this big,' and she indicated the length from elbow to finger tips.' Sharpen 'im real sharp on this rock.'

We'd sit cross-legged rubbing our sticks until they were sharp. Then off to scavenge in the earth around the trunk of the tree.

'Dig 'ere,' Maggie would tell me. Jenny and Randall knew already.

I'd dig with my stick in the earth and then follow down a tunnel to find a big very fat, white bodied, brown headed witchetty grub.

'E's a good un.' Maggie would encourage me because although I had eaten one I wasn't really crash hot keen on them and so I would give her mine.

Some days we found and killed snakes or even a cockatoo and we'd light a fire, roast and eat them. Maggie could rub sticks together to light a fire but now she mostly preferred matches.

We'd trap scrub turkeys, track down and eat honey ants, follow the birds to their nests for eggs, chew the sweet tips of grasses and dig for yams.

The Aboriginal men and women were endlessly kind, gentle and patient with the children, who were a bit spoiled by having someone to do everything for them e.g. picking up clothes, toys, getting a glass of water. Stan, of course, made sure they were acquiring skills as riders and farms skills. Lawrence was becoming a good rider from spending lots of time with Stan, riding with him in front on his saddle. Randall loved all sorts of machinery and Jenny loved to talk. Terri was still coughing and whooping and it was months ago that she had contracted whooping cough.

Our days made sense to us but not to others. Our days were numbered and eventually Stan caught up with this escapism and asked what his children were learning. I know now what it was but then I couldn't answer. For him, the classroom was the only place where learning could happen.

'Rosemary, the children are always outside, running wild, never in the classroom. This will have to stop. You are here to help them learn. You aren't to take them out any more.'

We all suffered from this. We were back into the four corrugated walls again to learn how to write pothooks, count to twenty and colour in without going over the lines and look at pictures of animals in the bush.

Hans had left. The baby Terri kept whooping most frighteningly and dreadfully and didn't seem to be getting better. At the table I'd be very worried as she tried to get her breath. She became more exhausted . . . The whooping cough had become chronic. Stan, although normally calm and even, was growing short-tempered. Mary looked very unhappy and chattered less. They took her to Hall's Creek, Derby and Wyndham hospitals for consultations.

Jean and Arthur sought more and more time together. They declared they were getting married. Stan told them, 'There is no accommodation here for a married couple.' I think there was another agenda but I never knew what it was. They decided to leave.

I didn't have any boyfriends here although I had had some boys ask me out in Sydney. I was quite sure I was terminally ugly, and that no one would want to approach me closely because they'd be put off by my ugliness.

Then one day after this situation had dribbled on for some weeks, Stan asked to see me after morning smoko.

'Terri Lorraine isn't getting any better so we have applied for leave because we need to see doctors at a big city hospital and we think we will apply for another post in Queensland closer to our families. We are leaving in four weeks when we get a relief manager. Rosemary, if you want to stay in the Kimberleys, then try the 7.00 am scheds for a few days and see if anyone else is looking for a governess.'

I stayed two months more. Once the children knew they were leaving they grew more restless and I started to lose motivation. But in the meantime, Tom Fisher, who had retired as manager from Wave Hill Station, arrived to act as relief manager.

The whole tone of the station changed as soon as Mary, Stan and the children left on the monthly ration plane. That was a great month.

Tom Fisher didn't care what I did. He was the caretaker. I woke early and sprinted down to the cattle yards where there was a big cut-out of clean skins and branded cattle. I spent the morning there on the gate to the crush. The men teased me and joked. I ate my lunch in the men's dining room and did some cooking with Henry and learned how to fire up the wood stoves with the right type and amount of wood. The afternoons I spent dreamily wandering along the creek often accompanied by piccaninnies and honing my bush skills. Sometimes I climbed a tree and sat there for ages just watching clouds, the movement of ants up and down the trunk and eyeing off the crows, ta-tah lizards and snakes. I read in the evenings – everything I could find.

It was a lazy, open, earth-oriented month of sun, sand and freedom. My soul was fed. The world felt perfectly in place.

Then I was offered a job as governess to John Langridge, the twelve-year-old son of Nan and Ron Langridge at Turkey Creek telegraph station. That is a different story.

Rosemary Morrow

BIOGRAPHIES

Sabine Erika: Born in Germany of German-Jewish parents, Sabine is a feminist, writes, travels and does drama with the intellectually disabled. She lives in Blackheath with her partner, Myra, and visits her eight grandchildren overseas and in Canberra from time to time.

Mira Sonik: Born in South Africa of Lithuanian-Latvian Jewish parents, Mira is a seeker after truths, a supporter of radical causes, and a devoted mother and grandmother. She lives in Katoomba in the Blue Mountains where she writes and cares for those in need.

Josephine Blanche Wolanski: Born in Sydney to Polish-Jewish immigrants. She lives by the bush in Mt. Victoria in the Blue Mountains with her daughter and many animals and is committed to her work in the human rights movement. Her interest in dance, music, art and the environment keeps her very busy.

Alison Gentle: Born in the USA, Allison is a teacher, student, parent and writer. She lives in Woodford in the Blue Mountains with her two children and is renovating a house there.

Rosemary Morrow: Born in Perth, seventh generation Australian of Irish and Greek descent, Rosemary has travelled widely in development work, written on permaculture and is passionate about caring for the earth. She lives in Katoomba in the Blue Mountains where she cares for her bit of the earth when she is not working for others.

Helena Wong: Born in New Zealand-Aotearoa of Finnish and Chinese parentage. Helena has always worked with words and language, first as a librarian and then in bookselling. Now she works as an information management consultant. Helena loves the bush and cares passionately about the environment and world peace. She lives in Leura in the Blue Mountains where she tends her garden and writes.